Democracy at Work

Patrick Burns, since co-authoring this book, has joined the TUC's Economic Department as a researcher. He has taught on shop-steward's courses and is former editor of *Bargaining Report*, a journal for trade union negotiators. He has written a number of articles and pamphlets on collective bargaining and trade union issues.

Mel Doyle has been active in trade union education since 1967 and is currently Assistant Secretary of the Workers' Educational Association. He has published a number of pamphlets, articles and reviews on historical and current trade union issues. With Peter Caldwell he co-edits *Trade Union Studies Journal*. He is co-author, with Nicholas McDonald, of *The Stresses of Work*.

Pan Trade Union Studies

Also available in this series

C. Aldred:
Women at Work

C. Baker and P. Caldwell:
Unions and Change Since 1945

A. Campbell and J. McIlroy:
Getting Organized

D. Eva and R. Oswald:
Health and Safety at Work

Series editors

Peter Caldwell
Tutor/Organizer
Workers' Educational Association
West Midlands

Alan Campbell
Lecturer in Industrial Relations
University of Liverpool

Mel Doyle
Assistant Secretary
Workers' Educational Association

Pan
Trade Union
Studies

Democracy at Work

Patrick Burns and Mel Doyle

Pan Original

Pan Books   London and Sydney

First published 1981 by Pan Books Ltd,
Cavaye Place, London SW10 9PG
© Patrick Burns and Mel Doyle and the Workers'
Educational Association 1981
ISBN 0 330 26478 8
Phototypeset by Input Typesetting Ltd,
London SW19 8DR
Printed in Great Britain by
Richard Clay (The Chaucer Press) Ltd,
Bungay, Suffolk

Contents

About the series

This series of books has been written for several groups of people
– those thinking of joining a union, or new members; those who
are just becoming active members; new and less experienced
shop-stewards; and indeed anyone interested in trade unions
today. It aims to provide an introduction to the principles of basic
trade unionism by discussing a wide range of arguments and
issues in the five key areas covered by the books. In
straightforward language each book points the way towards the
action that must be taken by individual trade unionists and by the
movement as a whole if their goals are to be achieved.

About this book

Most working people have little or no say in the organizations
they work for. Why is there so little democracy at work? Is it
because that's the only sensible way to run things, or are there
alternatives? And anyway, what do you gain from having a bigger
say over what management does? This book sets out to answer
those questions. It explains what 'participation', collective
bargaining and workers' control have to offer. It tells you the
things you ought to know about the organization you work for
and it gives you a practical guide to management and their
methods. And finally, it shows why building union organization
is the key to progress. The book offers no blueprint for democracy
at work, but after reading it you should have a clearer idea of the
facts, the arguments and the options.

Introduction

How much say do you have in the decisions which affect you at work? If you work for the average employer the answer is probably, 'Not much'. Maybe even, 'None'. Most workers don't get asked for their views before changes are made and don't hear about the more important decisions till *after* they've been taken. Think of a national work-force of around twenty million people and that's an awful lot of views being ignored, expertise being stifled and potential being wasted.

This book is about that problem – the problem of democracy at work, or rather the lack of it. It aims to show how things got that way, what the alternatives are, and how you can do something about it.

Our starting point is that there *are* alternatives, that work does not have to be run the way it is now. This book's view is that 'management's right to manage' can be challenged and that we don't have to accept it as the best way of running things. It's worth remembering that nineteenth century bosses claimed that union efforts to bargain about wages were a gross interference with their right to manage. Trade unions attacked that idea then, as they attack now the idea that managements should monopolize investment, planning and other big decisions. And as more and more jobs and living standards are put on the line, the demand for more democracy at work will grow. Putting your job in someone else's hands isn't such a safe bet in a recession.

Chapter one starts with the question of *why* democracy at work by doing two things: showing why workers have a right to more control at work, and why they need more say over what management does. Chapters two and three take a critical look at the organization you work for. In Chapter two we concentrate on your employer and the things you ought to know, but probably don't, about what he's doing.

Chapter three is a worker's guide to management: why it operates the way it does and how your job slots into management's view of the world. Chapter four looks at the battle to control and influence decision-making at work, and invites you to match your own experience against the examples we describe. Chapter five explains the steps you'll need to take to make sure you're organized enough to match the kind of resources management can muster against you. Lastly, Chapter six looks at the wider problems. It suggests that problems like unemployment, new technology, apathy and differing trade union approaches need not stifle the advance to democracy at work in the way the 'experts' predict.

Acknowledgements

A number of individuals have contributed to the preparation of this book: in particular Basil Bye, Lionel Fulton, Terry McDermott, Daniel Vulliamy, Stephen Wellings and Ann Zammit have offered valuable comments on various drafts of the manuscript. Our special thanks to Caroline Starkey for typing endless drafts without complaint.

Chapter **One**

Why democracy at work?

In this opening chapter we aim to do two things We show why workers have a right to more control over their work and their jobs. And we show why the fight for more democracy at work is worthwhile, why increasingly workers cannot afford to let management monopolize decision-making.

These are questions that are going to concern more and more workers as the economy becomes less and less able to guarantee them stable jobs and incomes. The way most companies, industries and services are run now is *not* the only way to run them – 'management's right to manage' was not one of the Ten Commandments. The alternative is for working people to increase the control they have over the organizations they work for. Reality being what it is, that is not going to mean instant workers' control or a sudden epidemic of worker cooperatives. In practical terms, what it *can* mean is:

● looking critically at how your workplace is run now;
● judging how big a say you and your union have in that process;
● building the alternatives from there.

The following chapters will be looking at these steps in detail. But first, back to the original question: what right have you as a worker to more control of work?

Is it any of your business?

Imagine that you've just won the pools. Not the stuff that headlines are made of, just a small fortune – say £50,000. You fancy making this wealth grow, but what do you do to make sure that it does? A spending spree has its attractions, but won't be much use to your kids in years to come. Putting it in a building society would be sensible, but that way you'll only just stay ahead of inflation. Finally you decide to follow in the footsteps of Marks and Spencer and go into business.

For the sake of argument let's say the business you choose is printing football pool coupons. A local bank helps you with a loan to buy in the hardware you need: printing machinery, folding and collating machinery, paper, inks and so on. To do the work you take on five employees.

Question 1 Leaving aside your bank loan, your £50,000 is on the starting blocks and raring to go. But unless you do all the work yourself, you're completely reliant on your employees to make it generate an income. You've provided the ignition, but your five printers are very definitely the engine. So who does the business 'belong' to?

In your first year of business, demand for football pool coupons hits an all-time high. By the end of the year you've sold £150,000 worth of coupons. Minus the £50,000 you spent on wages, bank interest, more paper, ink and other supplies, you're left with a profit, or surplus, of £100,000. That's on top of your original £50,000.

Question 2 Who does this £100,000 profit 'belong' to? You certainly got the business going but, as we've seen, it took your work-force to start it earning anything.

After the successful first year your printers put in a hefty wage claim. You reckon next year may be leaner and offer them half what they want. Their response is to join a union, which immediately asks you to negotiate a formal agreement on pay and other conditions, like safety. When you refuse, the printers walk off the job, and you give them all the sack. The union blacks their jobs, making it impossible for you to get replacements, and in the end you give in and take them back.

Question 3 Is this an unfair use of union power? Even though you were perfectly within your legal rights to sack the five, the union used the closed shop and its control of jobs to make you back down.

After this experience, you decide to get tough in a different way. You hire a supervisor to chase up hard on things like timekeeping, absenteeism, speed and quality of work. You accept the supervisor's suggestion that productivity will be improved if each employee sticks to one task – instead of all five swapping tasks from time to time.

Question 4 This is good firm management and provided the workers accept it, it will probably improve productivity. But what about jobs becoming more boring, and who will the productivity savings 'belong' to?

After a time another local printer offers to buy you out. He's particularly interested in your machinery and premises but doesn't plan to keep on any of your staff. You sell the business for £250,000, of which a total of £30,000 – £5000 each – goes to the staff in redundancy payments.

Question 5 The amount you sell the business for is far more than the £50,000 you started it with. Yet virtually all the extra goes to you and not to the work-force whose labour partly created it. In any case did you have the right to sell the business without consulting your work-force?

Business and the snowball effect

By now it's pretty obvious we could use this example to work our way through most of the situations you come across at work. But the story we've developed so far already has in it the themes we want to develop in this book.

What we have described is a mini-version of the way business works in Britain. It may look a crude example, but we challenge any industrialist to show that it's inaccurate. The economy of this country is still dominated by companies: they employ 70 per cent of the labour force compared to the 30 per cent who work in hospitals, nationalized industries and the rest of the public sector. Companies are started with the money put up by individuals, who then get a stake – or a *share* – in the company. However massive and complex the biggest firms like ICI, GEC and others may look, they all started in this way as one or more companies. And the law of the land makes it quite clear that companies and what they produce belong to the shareholders, not to their workers. Think back to how you answered Question 1: is the law right to create a master-and-servant set-up as soon as a company is formed?

Next, think back to your first year of trading as a pools coupon printer. As we showed, putting up the money to start a business is only switching on the ignition. Without a work-force there is no engine to make everything move. And that of course has implications for any profits the firm makes: that is the income that remains once wages and other costs have been paid. Any company accountant will explain to you that a firm's profit is spent in the way the directors, on behalf of the shareholders, decide. It is literally the property of the company's owners. But as our story showed, that profit is only possible through the efforts of the work-force.

Is the comparison unfair – what about the giant companies

whose enormous investment programmes do as much as the work-force to generate profits? The answer to this is that companies that are giants now are simply the product of generations of wealth created in exactly the same way: the original injection of money plus the efforts of workers down the years. If two people start a snowball rolling downhill it would be ridiculous for one of them to claim responsibility for the majority of snow it picked up on the way down. Yet property and company law do just that, by acting as though one side only – the shareholders – have been involved in the process.

The trade union case for more democracy at work goes to the very heart of the way businesses are run. It starts from the fact that the economic system, backed up by the legal system, creates a power pyramid with shareholders at the top and workers at the bottom – even though workers physically produce the wealth that fuels the system.

By referring to 'wealth producing' we're certainly not just talking about workers who physically make products for sale. We're talking about everybody who's employed in the economy whether they work in manufacturing, in shops, in local government, in hospitals, in distribution and the rest. In all of these the end-product, whatever it is, depends as much on the labour force as on whoever provides the financial spark. As far as this basic right to control over the decisions that affect you is concerned, the position is the same whether you work in the private sector or the public sector. In fact, as we suggest in a special section on page 49, the public sector is a step nearer to such control as far as ownership is concerned – but what about the problem of management?

Management's right to manage

The ownership system we've described above has existed for well over 200 years. Not surprisingly in that time it has developed a method of management to match. A system that puts all ownership rights in the hands of the shareholders automatically gives them control over the people they employ. Modern management methods reflect that fact. Management is simply the agent of the owners – put there to carry out their policies and get their decisions accepted.

Go back to your answers to Questions 3 and 4: the ones about trade union action against dismissals and supervision of jobs. As a businessman you had every right to take the action the story suggested. More than that, your action was a classic expression – one of them – of management's right to manage. But is this the way organizations should be run? As we suggest in Chapter four, this is not the *only* form management need take. As a recent book describing workers' co-operatives put it:

The concept here is that management is simply a skill, like welding or draughtsmanship, and does not denote rank in a hierarchy, nor the right to power except in so far as it is delegated to the manager by the work-force.
Workers Co-operatives, Aberdeen People's Press

The alternative is the system we are lumbered with at present. Take a look at one of its by-products.

The trouble flared in the mail order department, which was under the direct supervision of Mr Malcolm Alden – thirty-two years old and in that very month appointed a director. Mr Devshi Bhudia, aged nineteen, was a worker in the department. His task that day was to sort thirteen crates of outgoing mail for dispatch by the evening post. He expressed his resentment at being put in charge of some three or four student workers on the job: if he was to be in charge, he wanted more money, but Mr Alden said firmly, 'No.' Mr Bhudia also felt the job, with its time limit, was an unfair imposition. He, therefore, and his colleagues, who sympathized with him, 'went slow'. Mr Alden noticed it: there was a scene when Mr Alden asked what was going on. Mr Alden there and then dismissed him. He left: and the three (or four – the exact number is in doubt) students, who were working with him, walked out with him. There was an element of premeditation in Mr Bhudia's departure. He had become discontented with pay and conditions and a week earlier had discussed with some the possibility of joining a union. He had carried his dissatisfaction sufficiently far to seek and obtain the promise of a job elsewhere before, on his own admission, he provoked the incident which brought about his dismissal. After he and his three or four sympathizers had walked out, they remained in the street outside the factory until seven p.m. They were still there when Mrs Jayaben Desai and her son, Sunil, also walked out at some time between six and seven p.m.

The above extract could describe the beginnings of countless disputes up and down the country. There is nothing remotely extraordinary about it; simply a case of an order not being obeyed, new work methods being imposed, and management hostility to the union. Fairly similar, in fact, to the situation we put you in as a pools coupon printer (see Questions 3 and 4). As it happens, the extract we've quoted describes the start of one of the most well-known disputes in Britain this century: Grunwick. The quote is from an official report into the dispute. All that made the Grunwick case extraordinary was the lengths the workers and their union were prepared to go to resist 'management's right to manage'. There are not 'Grunwicks' every week of the year because management control is the norm and it's more often accepted than not for a variety of reasons: fear of job loss; fear of losing pay; or simply the successful negotiating of shop-stewards.

Your job in their hands

We all pay for our lack of control over management decisions by effectively putting our jobs in their hands. Below are three examples of management's right to manage in action, the first from the baking group Spillers-French (now part of Dalgety).

Spillers-French have gone out of the breadmaking business and 8,000 redundant workers have not even had the required ninety days' notice for consultations by the unions involved.

Hundreds of USDAW Scottish Bakers Section members are affected in the closed bakeries at Dumfries and Stevenston, Ayrshire, as well as many USDAW members in Manchester, Plymouth and South Wales who work on the distribution side.

Hundreds more Scottish Bakers production-workers are expected to bake more bread to make up for the loss of three units north of the border. There seems little chance of finding many extra bakery jobs in the West of Scotland, however.

In England, USDAW transport members are being transferred from Spillers employment to Ranks or Allied Bakeries at some of the thirteen plants sold to the two remaining big bakery firms. But their jobs are only being guaranteed for twelve months.

Shocked and angry officials and shop-stewards from USDAW and other unions only learnt of the closure of the twenty-three bakeries at the same time as the public announcement – just a fortnight before the axe was due to fall.

Since then, a top level Union deputation, including USDAW National Officer Mr Gerald Kiely, has been to see the responsible Government Ministers, Agriculture Minister Mr John Silkin and Prices Secretary Mr Roy Hattersley, only to discover that even the Government had not been consulted in time to consider saving the Spillers bread operation.

In fact, Ministers were only informed on a confidential basis by the Bank of England that Spillers-French would collapse totally unless the Government would agree to the sale of the thirteen bakeries for £15½ million to Rank Hovis McDougall and Associated British Foods (Allied Bakeries) in a matter of days without a reference to the Monopolies Commission.

Dawn, USDAW, May 1978

The second example concerns one of the Northern Engineering Industries (NEI) companies in the North East:

> Rumours that NEI Reyrolle at Hebburn were really planning to make 1000 workers redundant two months ago, when 500 redundancies were announced, have now been squashed. Alas the rumours are fact. Reyrolles new Managing Director, Colonel 'Polly' Perkins, speaking at what one shop-steward described as the most brutal meeting he had ever attended, informed the shop-stewards that a further 450 jobs are to go on top of the 500 by December of this year.
>
> Colonel Perkins was brought into Reyrolles to replace the former Managing Director, G. B. Tully, following last years bitter AUEW-TASS strike which lasted nine weeks! It is now clear he was brought in by the parent company NEI as a hard man to carry out a drastic programme of rationalization.
>
> TUSIU *Bulletin*, January 1979

Earlier in the same year the Trade Union Studies Information Unit reported the way Vickers were planning to cut jobs:

At the beginning of the New Year, Vickers Ltd, the giant heavy engineering company with long traditional associations with Tyneside announced the intended closure of one of its three engineering works along Scotswood Road in Newcastle. In a public letter to its employees the company told 750 workers at the Scotswood Works that it intended to close the factory between March and September 1979.

In the letter, Mr Noel Davies, Joint Managing Director of Vickers Ltd, concluded with a thinly veiled threat to other Vickers plants in an attempt to pre-empt any collective, united stand over the closure proposals. He said:

It is with great regret that the management has had to take this most unpalatable decision having had such a long association with the activities of these particular works.

The company recognizes the need to maximize employment opportunities but at the same time it cannot ignore the realities of life that jobs can be protected only on the basis of commercially viable business. If decisions are taken in the short term to preserve jobs at all costs, other businesses where jobs are currently secure would be put in jeopardy.

Peter Tolchard, Convener at the Scotswood Works, publicly attacked the lack of consultation by management concerning their decision and already a growing protest campaign is being organized by the Vickers workers. A campaign committee has been set up by shop-stewards with two representatives from the other five Vickers works on Tyneside plus one representative from each of the eight unions at the Scotswood works. The first meeting of this committee took place on 9 January and it is intended to meet weekly on Tuesdays to organize the fight against the closures.

TUSIU *Bulletin*, January 1979

As in the case of the early simmerings at Grunwick, there is nothing exceptional about these examples. Possibly the job cuts were announced more brutally than normal, but that is not the point. What the examples do have in common is the bosses' ability to sack labour in precisely the same way they can sell off machines. Turn back to the story and to Question 5 for how this process looks when it's put in simple terms. Is it any wonder that trade unionists have campaigned for generations against the system of ownership that allows wealth producers (workers) to be treated in this way?

This is all theory – what about practicalities?

So far we've concentrated on the way the business system works and the implications it has for management methods. The actual examples we've quoted have all been dramatic ones and show employers and management in the worst possible light. What about the argument that reality isn't like that? In any case, as far as many workers are concerned the *less* they know about what management is doing the better.

In the next part of this chapter we aim to show that this view is wrong. We shall show why workers have a crucial stake in all decisions employers take, and why it is essential that workers have much more control over those decisions. But first think about the types of decision that are taken which affect you.

Your employer takes two sorts of decisions:

- those that affect you *directly*;
- those that affect you *indirectly*.

Literally hundreds of decisions could be listed under each heading. Below we give just a few examples.

'Direct effect' decisions   Here are three decisions which every employer makes. These are areas over which every employer must have a *policy*:

- how much to pay you;
- how many hours you should work;

● what speed you ought to work at.

In all three cases it's obvious that you're going to feel the immediate effect of what the boss decides. You'll notice from:

● the amount of money you have to spend;
● how much leisure time you've got;
● how tired you are at the end of the week.

Now assume that you and your union have *no say at all* in these matters. Your employer is free to do as he wants. In other words, the boss decides entirely for himself what to pay you, how long you'll work, and how fast you'll work. Most working people – certainly those in unions – would be appalled at such an idea. This is because most employers must now *bargain* about these vital matters with a trade union that represents their workers. The decision in fact becomes a two-way process: two sides are involved before a decision, or agreement, is finally arrived at. But as a companion volume in this series – *Unions and Change Since 1945* – shows, this wasn't always the case in the past. As recently as the end of the last century, these vital decisions about wage packets and hours of work were mainly a one-way process. The boss decided and you accepted – or you lost your job.

Things only changed because workers formed unions to collectively represent their interests and forced employers to bargain with them on basic bread-and-butter issues. A totally undemocratic way of reaching decisions gave way to a more democratic one – because workers affected by decisions began to have some say in them.

Some employers seem to regret the passing of those days. But the majority no longer expect to be able to fix pay and hours and job speeds without first bargaining about them with trade unions.

'Indirect effect' decisions   Now let's look at some decisions where the effect is less obvious, where the employer is deciding:

● how much to spend on installing new machinery;
● whether to buy up a local firm that competes with yours;

● whether to open up a new factory abroad.

The impact of these decisions will take longer to filter down to the shop-floor. But it's very much a question of *when* and not *if* you're going to be affected. Let's take each decision in turn.

The decision about new machinery   In most industries new designs are producing more efficient machines all the time. If your boss doesn't keep up with these improvements he won't be the only one to lose out. You will as well. If his competitors put in new machinery that helps do the job better and quicker they'll start to sell their products cheaper. Other things being equal, that will mean that your employer will find it harder to sell his goods or services. Who buys the more expensive goods when they don't have to? If your employer is selling fewer products and making less money then one option becomes more and more attractive – saving money by sending workers down the road.

For example, take the case of the car company BL (formerly British Leyland). After a major investigation into the firm's problems in 1975 the Ryder Report concluded that:

In the automotive industry, most manufacturing equipment is replaced after eight to twelve years. In BL more than half the machines and equipment are over fifteen years old.

The Ryder Report made it clear that this was a big factor in Leyland's falling share of the British car market. It recommended that: 'A massive programme to modernize plant and equipment at BL must be put in hand immediately.'

What was the result of BL's short-sightedness? Between 1970 and 1980 its market share slumped by more than half from 39 per cent to 18 per cent. In the same period a staggering 48,000 jobs were lost. Would BL workers have been as careless as management were with their job prospects if they had been consulted about investment plans in the first place?

The decision about buying up another firm   A glance at the financial pages of your daily paper will show you how often one firm buys up another (a *takeover*), or joins forces with

25

another on equal footing (a *merger*). Such decisions are frequently followed by what accountants have been known to call *rationalization*. In practical terms this can often mean job cuts, especially if the two firms are in the same business. Even where two quite different firms merge, the new boss may use the opportunity the upheaval provides to 'slim down' the work-force.

One of the classic examples of this was provided by GEC's takeover of AEI and merger with English Electric in the late 1960s. In 1967 when the three companies were still separate, they employed a total of 268,000 workers. Four years later, after a series of cut-throat boardroom battles, the now combined companies employed 225,000 – a rationalization of more than 40,000 jobs!

The decision about opening a factory abroad   At first sight this might appear an obscure, almost irrelevant decision. It will involve complicated financial manoeuvrings, possibly thousands of miles away. But again it's just a matter of time before you and your fellow workers feel the effect.

Take the case of Lucas Industries, a company which makes components for the motor industry. Between 1973–4 and 1978–9 Lucas increased its overseas work-force from 12,600 to 18,400. In the same period it cut its British work-force from 71,700 to 69,100. 5800 jobs created abroad, and 2600 lost in Britain in just five years.

We have given three examples of the effects company decision-making can have on workers – BL's failure to replace worn-out machines, GEC's decision to swallow two rivals and spit out 40,000 jobs, and Lucas's decision to create jobs abroad and chop them at home. All three decisions have one thing in common. They were taken without any serious discussion with those most affected – the workers.

These examples reflect no more than a tiny proportion of the decisions an employer takes in any one year. The total list would be endless (indeed many of these 'other' decisions are discussed in the following chapters). We are not suggesting that the effects are always going to be as serious as these three examples. They have been chosen simply to emphasize that, however remote your employer's decisions may seem, they will (sooner or later) affect you and your workmates.

In this chapter we've argued that you have a right to a say in the decisions managements take, and that you have a stake in those decisions – a stake that could be your job and your income. In Chapter two we turn to the first steps you can take to extend your influence, and the union's influence, at work.

Further reading

Four books or pamphlets that make useful background reading to this chapter are:

Democracy at Work (BBC/TUC/WEA, 1977).

Industrial Democracy (TUC, 1979).

C. Baker and P. Caldwell *Unions and Change Since 1945* (Pan Books, 1981), in the same series as this book.

Industrial Democracy (Transport and General Workers' Union, 1978).

Chapter **Two**

Knowing your employer

In the first chapter we made the case for more democracy at work. We also showed that workers more often than not have a very big stake in the decisions that management take. In doing this we've clearly begged a big question, namely: so what do we do about it.

This chapter, and the ones that follow it, set out to answer that question. Our starting point is this: you need to know the organization you're dealing with before you can mount an effective challenge to the way it controls your working life. Without knowledge about how and why employers and managements operate, the different forms this can take, and their different strengths and weaknesses, you will be trying to negotiate a maze without ever finding the entrance.

To provide the kind of basic knowledge you need, we deal with your employer and your management separately. This chapter looks at who owns the organization you work for: your employer. Chapter three looks at who runs it day-to-day: your management. Chapters four and five go on to build on this information to suggest the kind of action you can take to extend democracy at work and get more control over the decisions that affect you.

The type of organization you work for has a major bearing on the way you'll go about extending democracy at work. Because different organizations are financed and managed in quite different ways there cannot be one simple blueprint. For this reason we shall deal with the different types of employing organizations separately.

The vast majority of working people in Britain are employed by one of three kinds of organization:

- a company;
- a nationalized industry or public corporation;
- local or national government (including the Health Service).

About seventeen million are employed in companies, two million in nationalized industries and state corporations, and five million in local/national government and the NHS. In addition there are a relatively small number who work for partnerships, charities, voluntary groups and so on.

We start with the sector that employs the biggest share of Britains work-force: companies. The non-company sector – the NHS, the Civil Service and so on – is dealt with on page 49.

Companies

Roughly seven out of every ten workers in Britain are employed by a company. Virtually all the 690,000 or so companies are known as *limited liability companies* – the word Limited appears at the end of their name. This means that the owners of the firm are protected if the business fails. Instead of having to hand over every penny the firm owes, their liability, or responsibility, is limited to the value of the *shares* in the company. The owners of the company are the *shareholders*.

There are two basic types of company, private companies and public companies.

A typical *private company* is owned by half a dozen or so shareholders, all of whom, or most of whom, are also *directors*. In other words there is practically no gap between *ownership* and *control*: the people who own the firm also take the decisions about the way its run.

A *public company*, as the name suggests, is one where the public are free to purchase shares. A public company therefore may have thousands or even millions of shares, and a correspondingly large number of shareholders. It would be wrong to imagine that ordinary individuals own all these shares. A large and growing proportion of shares in public companies are owned by organizations like banks, insurance companies, and pension funds. The directors of companies in this position often own some of the shares, but rarely enough to actually control a majority. So in public companies the owners of the firm (the shareholders), by and large, are not automatically the people who *control* it. You can find out if your company is a public company by looking it up in the *Stock Exchange Yearbook*. We explain where you can get hold of this and other reference books on pages 53–6.

We now come back to the process of building up your knowledge about your employer, the entrance to the maze, as it were. As a starting point, see what your answers are to the following four questions.

Question 1 Do you know exactly who *owns* the company you work for?

Question 2 Do you know what other business *activities* or *interests* your company has?

Question 3   Do you know what state your company's *finances* are really in?

Question 4   Broadly speaking, are you confident you know what your company's *plans* are?

If you are not a company director and answered yes to any of these, you're either amazingly lucky or amazingly over-confident. The vast majority of British companies treat se-crecy as a way of life where the work-force is concerned. The general rule is: the more vital a piece of information is to the job and income security of workers, the less they ought to know about it – at least until after decisions have been made. If you think that's an exaggeration, think of how you an-swered the four questions above. In the sections that follow we look at the questions separately and in detail to show that you *do* need to know the answers to them.

Who is your employer?

This may appear to be a simple question to answer. In fact it is often a surprisingly complicated problem. It also helps demonstrate why it is so vital that trade unionists have a thorough knowledge of the organization they work for.

To illustrate the problem let's take five firms making car components in the Midlands.

Smiths Axles Ltd is a one-off firm. Its small handful of shares are owned by the boss and his wife who are the only direc-tors. If you're aiming for a say in this company's decisions, you won't need to look far to find out who's in control.

Midland Motors (Birmingham) Ltd is owned by another firm, called the *parent company*. The parent company owns two more factories in the neighbourhood and one of its directors is also on the board of your firm.

In this situation it is more difficult for you to influence decisions which affect your workplace. The main problem is that those who make the day-to-day decisions in your firm are *not* necessarily the people who make the key decisions about the *group* of companies of which your firm is only part. The management in your factory could be as much in the dark as you about what plans the top company has. To have a say in those plans you'll need to negotiate with the firm that owns yours – the parent company.

AEL Components Ltd is owned by a large group of companies. It's just one part – the motor components division – of a parent company, the *Automotive Engineering Ltd* group, with other engineering interests. The parent company has its head office in London.

In addition *AEL Components Ltd* itself owns two smaller firms which are termed *subsidiary companies*. Because it's in the middle – owning subsidiaries, but owned itself by a parent company – *AEL Components Ltd* can be termed an *intermediate*.

This will again affect your response as a trade unionist. You are now dealing with a parent company producing more than one set of products, operating in different parts of the country.

British Vehicles (Midlands) Ltd is similar to *AEL Components Ltd*, but with one big difference. Its parent company also has a division abroad – a *foreign subsidiary*. This makes the parent company a *multinational*, a firm with subsidiaries in more than one country.

This is an important extra dimension for trade unionists. For example your multinational parent company may expect many benefits from abroad: different tax laws, weaker unions, fewer employment rights. It may begin to think in terms of replacing some of its UK subsidiaries with more foreign ones. The Lucas Industries example we quoted on page 26 is only one of many. All the more reason to be aware of your firm's links.

American Systems (UK) is similar again, but with a further important difference. *American Systems (UK)*'s parent company is not British, but based abroad (in the USA in this example). Otherwise the structure is the same, a head office controlling intermediates that each have their own subsidiaries.

This final example highlights the importance of knowing who exercises ultimate control over your firm. Just think of the futility of trying to negotiate seriously with an employer like *American Systems (UK)* about long term plans that in reality are decided way above his head on the other side of the Atlantic.

In Chapters four and five we examine how trade unionists can deal effectively with these kinds of problems. But first we look at how you can find out who your employer is. It is not possible in this short book to give a full guide to company financial structures. Here we do no more than consider some of the major items in company accounts, which hopefully will give you at least a working profile of the firm you work for. We also tell you *where* you can find the information (you will find a checklist of these sources of information on pages 53–6).

Getting information on ownership   To find out who owns your company you need to know who owns the shares. Companies must submit this information in an Annual Return to the Registrar of Companies at least once a year. This document is filed in Cardiff, with a copy in London, and any member of the public can see it for a small fee. Scottish companies Returns are filed in Edinburgh. In any detective work you do on your company it's important that you know the firm's full name. With nearly 700,000 companies in business you'll quickly get lost in the filing index if, say, you try to find Davies and Son when you ought to be looking for Davis and Son. The Annual Return reveals the names and addresses of a company's shareholders. If you work for a small company this will tell you at a glance who the owners are.

But as we said earlier the larger public companies often have hundreds of shareholders. If you don't find the Annual Return useful then you can try the company's Annual Accounts which are also filed with the Registrar of Companies in London, Cardiff and Edinburgh. The accounts give a mass of useful information which we refer to several times in this chapter. On the question of ownership they reveal two helpful things:

- The *Directors' Report* section of the accounts must show anybody who owns 5 per cent or more of the shares.
- The *Notes to the Accounts* must give the name of the *ultimate holding company*, i.e. the parent company at the top of the pyramid of subsidiary companies.

Other useful information provided in the Accounts includes the names of your company's directors with details of how many shares they own. That will tell you whether the people who run your company also own it.

A major weakness of company law is that it doesn't make firms reveal the finances for individual plants. Countless shop-stewards have been frustrated to find that they can get hold of the figures for their parent company, but not the figures that matter – the ones on the plant or site they work at.

If you can't get to Companies House offices there are other sources of information you can use. A publication called *Who Owns Whom?* gives details of the ownership of public and larger private companies. If your company is a public company whose shares are traded or quoted on the Stock Exchange you'll find it listed in the *Stock Exchange Yearbook*. Both these books are extremely useful but very expensive. A cheaper option is to try your local reference library.

If your company is a public company then you can get it to send you a copy of the Annual Report it sends to all its shareholders. This is usually a glossy published version of the accounts the firm has to file at Companies House – and the information it contains is identical.

Finally, if your union has a research office they should be able to supply the details you want. Alternatively, the Labour Research Department carries out research on companies for its affiliates. See pages 53–6 for notes on all the sources mentioned in this section.

What are your company's activities and interests?

Having sorted out who owns your company it's a logical second step to make sure you know what else the firm makes, owns or has a stake in. Clearly you will know what goes on at your own workplace. But the different sorts of company structure we illustrated on page 31 show your boss could have a lot of irons in the fire.

Let's take a practical example of why this matters to you as a trade unionist. Suppose you work as a print worker for the *Daily Express* and negotiate about wages on behalf of your fellow print workers. In negotiations you'll sit opposite *Daily Express* management – but as a trade unionist that's not all you need to know. For a start the *Daily Express* is owned by a company called Express Newspapers Ltd which also owns the *Daily Star*, the London *New Standard* and the *Sunday Express*. But even Express Newspapers Ltd is not the top company in the pyramid. It's only a tiny part of a much larger company – called Trafalgar House Ltd – the *ultimate holding company* as we explained earlier. Trafalgar House Ltd owns more than newspapers; it owns companies in the building, shipping and leisure industries. Express Newspapers is only one part of Trafalgar House's Newspapers and Magazines Group, which itself accounts for a mere 20 per cent or so of Trafalgar Houses income. Why does this matter? If you are a union representative for *Daily Express* print workers, knowing what set-up you're part of helps you because:

● You might be able to improve the members pay by claiming 'parity' with workers at another of Express Newspapers Ltd's papers.
● You'll know that, whatever your management say about what the *Daily Express* can afford to pay you, you're part of a giant group whose profits run into millions of pounds.
● On the other hand you'll also be aware that newspapers are a dangerously small part of the top company's interests. Closing down the *Daily Express*, or selling it off, might not damage Trafalgar House too much.

These are only a few examples of how you can make practical

use of knowledge about your company's interests. Even if it turns out you're employed by a one-off company – with no subsidiaries and no parent – it will have been worth checking. It will help you make sensible comparisons with other firms' wages, give you an idea of how long the boss could put up with a strike, and so on.

Getting information on activities and interests   If your firm is part of a group of companies, start by looking at the annual report of the parent company (the published version, or the one filed at Companies House – see page 53). In the annual report the top company must give the names of the major companies it owns – its *subsidiaries*. This information is usually towards the back of the document. If the group has subsidiaries in different industries it may print the subsidiaries in batches according to which industry or division they are in.

If you're lucky this section may also give the addresses of all the subsidiaries, so that you can contact the shop-steward(s) there (see Chapter five for more on this tactic).

If you can't get a copy of the annual report in either of the ways suggested above look up the name of the top company (the ultimate holding company) in *Who Owns Whom?*. If it's there, all subsidiaries will be listed.

If your firm isn't owned by another, checking on its interests is easier. In the Directors' Report section of the annual report and accounts (usually near the beginning) the company must say what its main activities are. At least this ought to give you an idea of whether the company has any significant business beyond what goes on at your own workplace. And if there are subsidiaries, remember they ought to be listed. Some companies will go a bit further than just listing their main activities and break these down in terms of size. The rubber and plastics firm, British Vita Ltd, is one example. Its Annual Report gives a useful breakdown of what the work-force produces, and by the market they sell in:

Table 1

By product	£m	By market	percentage
Cellular foam	28	Furniture	29
Industrial rubber compounds and components	15	General industry	24
		Household textiles and consumer	19
Fibre and fabric processing	10	Transportation	13
Consumer	7	Bedding	6
Service	6	Other	9
	66		100

This small extra feature could be one more snapshot which helps the company's workers build up a full picture of their employer's interests. The information could stand you in good stead. If the accounts showed that the division you worked in was losing its share of output to another division, you would have advance warning of a threat to jobs.

Two other areas that should be checked out are the directors' interests and any overseas activities the company may have.

It's worth knowing how many pies the directors have their fingers in. It's not unknown for directors of one company to do themselves a favour by placing contracts with a second company that they happen to be directors of. More seriously, you might find work being sub-contracted out to another firm where a similar link exists. Any other directorships your own directors hold must be listed in the Annual Return filed at Companies House. A shortcut is a publication called *Directory of Directors*. A good many, though not all, directors list their directorships in this publication and it should be in your local reference library.

The steps we've recommended above will help you get a view of your firm's interests in this country. But what about the foreign dimensions? The sources of information already referred to can help you in a couple of ways on this score. In the first place, some of the goods you produce may be sold overseas. The value of these exports must appear in the Directors' Report if your firm's sales here and abroad total more than 1 million.

Knowing your company has markets overseas is important to the profile of its business you are building up. Even more important is the question of what it actually produces there. We mentioned the case of Lucas Industries earlier as a firm who had built up their production abroad at the expense of jobs in Britain. Surprisingly, given the importance of this side of the company's operations, the usual sources won't give you much help in finding out about this overseas production. Companies quoted on the Stock Exchange – public companies – are subject to one fairly tight requirement (though it's not legally binding). The Stock Exchange itself requires any public company carrying on at least a tenth of its business abroad to give a geographical breakdown. This should be in the annual report and is usually found towards the front. But it doesn't have to be on a country-by-country basis so you may find a list of sales in, say, Asia, Australasia, and Europe. The more helpful reports do break down their foreign production by country and sometimes by product.

What are the finances like?

This book is not a guide to company accounts, so we are not about to launch into explanations of liquidity ratios, current cost accounting, or value added. In this chapter the aim is to show why some basic knowledge gives you powerful back-up in your dealings with your employer.

Where the firm's ownership and interests are concerned, some workers are always going to argue that ignorance is bliss. There's often a strong feeling that those are questions better left to management and their accountants. But when it comes to the firm's finances you literally can't afford to be in the dark. Take the most obvious example: the annual wage claim. And then imagine lodging it without having a clue what financial state the company is in. These will be some of your problems:

- You'll have no facts to fight with if management offer you a lot less on the grounds that the firm '. . . can't afford it'.
- If you accept, and the next week the local paper reports your firm's record profits, you'll look an idiot.
- If you reject the offer and make a fight of it, and the firm turns out to be on the rocks, you risk putting yourself and your mates out of work.
- If management realize they can exploit your ignorance in one way, they'll soon think of other ways on other topics.

These points should make it obvious that knowledge is power. If management have a monopoly of knowledge you're that much weaker; if you have a good clear picture of where the firm stands you're in a stronger position to represent your members. And another point is worth stressing. It's mistaken to think of using knowledge in this way purely defensively. A football team that knows the opposition's strengths and weaknesses inside out isn't just equipped to stop them scoring – it ought to be able to launch a few attacks as well.

In your relations with management that broadly means taking the initiative, making a far stronger case, and standing a correspondingly better chance of getting what the members are after. Consider the way the union side of the Ford national joint negotiating committee presented a wage claim in 1977. This is a small extract from the claim:

Ford UK's performance and prospects

The Accounts for 1976 show a remarkable increase in Group sales from £1,146.5 million in 1975 to £1,627.5 million in 1976. Over the same period pre-tax profits (after allowing for depreciation, and after writing off all research and development costs) rose from £14.1 million to £121.6 million. What are the realities behind such figures?

First of all, it seems clear that Ford made a remarkable recovery from the recession of 1975, one that was dramatically better than the rest of the UK vehicle industry. The official Index of Industrial Production shows the output of the vehicle industry no higher in 1976 than in 1975. On a crude count of passenger car and CV production the unit total only increased by 3.4 per cent. By contrast Ford's vehicle units sold increased by 110,000 to 644,000, or by just over 20 per cent.

Thus Ford has been strongly increasing its share of UK production. The SMMT data show Ford as accounting for 28.74 per cent of UK passenger car production in 1976, and 38.06 per cent of CV production. Back in 1974 the proportions had only been 25 per cent for passenger cars, and 32.6 per cent for CVs.

Of course, Ford UK's real output consists of more than vehicles. It would be helpful to have from the company more adequate information about the advance of its component sales, in real terms. But there seems no reason to suppose that the prices of Ford's component sales rose faster between 1975 and 1976 than the prices of manufacturing output generally (an increase of 16.4 per cent). Assuming that the overall price increase on Ford's sales between 1975 and 1976 was around 17 per cent, the *volume* increase was 20 per cent or slightly more.

This is just half of the first page of a forty-five-page document lodged along with the pay claim in that year. The union side's relative success over the years in pay negotiations with Ford is acknowledged throughout the motor industry.

This is not to say that claims like the Ford one are essential whatever the circumstances. The Ford union side have to deal with a giant multinational company worth millions of dollars worldwide. Obviously they can't submit their pay claim on the back of an envelope and hope to be taken seriously. In fact, that claim was drawn up with the help of the Transport and General Workers Union research department; the Trade Union Research Unit at Ruskin College, Oxford; and the city stockbrokers, Philips & Drew Ltd.

The kind of information you should be looking for will obviously be scaled down to the kind of situation you're in. If there's only £25 in the shop-stewards' fund, Philips & Drew will be a bit beyond your means in any case. But the approach of the Ford unions is worth working towards. So how can you check out the firm's finances without spending too much time and money?

Getting information on the finances Checking the finances is a question of how far you want to go. Both the firm's ownership and interests are a (fairly) open and shut case – once you've got your hands on the facts. The annual accounts, for example, will tell you quickly the names of any parent company and subsidiaries.

But with the finances, the problems only really start when you've managed to get the facts. Here, the facts will not automatically speak for themselves.

One way or another your job is to beat a path through the jargon to find out what sort of financial position your firm is really in. There are three ways you can go about it.

Check the financial press It's no good relying on the money pages of tabloid national papers like the *Mail* or the *Express* and certainly not the *Sun* or the *Mirror*. The *Financial Times* reports on the latest results from the bigger companies six days a week. Find out when your firm's are due and see

41

what the *FT* says about them. The *Investors' Chronicle* comes out once a week and can be used in the same way. Your local paper(s) might report company results, and if they don't you could encourage them to start. Doing it this way means the verdict on your firm will be fairly general – but if the option is no information at all the effort is worthwhile.

Get the experts to help　Let's assume you want more than a three-line summary of how the firm is doing – but not more than a couple of pages of explanation you can understand. It makes sense to seek advice that's sympathetic – trade union orientated in other words. A starting point is your own union – especially if it has a research department. Failing that there is the independent Labour Research Department. Both can give you summary reports of your employer's latest financial position (see page 55). Two other options are friendly academics, or local trade union research units like the ones in Coventry, Southampton, Leeds and Newcastle – all of whom you could contact through your local trades council.

You could try one of the commercial company services, but most of them are too expensive and too keen to tell you things you don't need to know. An exception is the Extel service which will send you an information sheet on just your firm. This will contain a lot of financial data from which you can pick and choose the stuff you want.

Do it yourself　Not as daunting as it sounds – depending how far you want to go. Below we have listed five items that will give you a quick sketch-map of the finances. If you want to go deeper into the subject, page 56 recommends some handbooks that provide a thorough guide – for trade unionists, not trainee accountants – to company accounts.

The five key items we have selected will all appear in your firm's annual accounts (see page 53 for how to get them). The pages from the ERF Holdings Ltd accounts on pages 43, 44 and 45 show where the figures you want appear in the accounts.

The *sales* figure is a fair guide to how the company is doing, provided you take more than one years figures. The accounts always provide a two year comparison and previous copies

Report of the directors

The directors present their report for the fifty two weeks ended 29th March 1980.

Group profits
The profit before taxation was £4.303m. compared with £3.342m. last year.
The profit retained in the group was £3.736m., the comparative for last year being £2.942m.

Dividends
An interim ordinary dividend of 2.1 pence was paid on 29th January 1980.
The directors recommend a final dividend for the period ended 29th March 1980 of 2.1 pence.
The total ordinary dividend will then be 4.2 pence (gross equivalent 6.0 pence).
The accounts also provide for a full year's preference dividend at 10 pence per share.

Issue of shares
During the 1979 conversion period 210,582 shares were issued to holders of £118,000 loan stock. This gave rise to share premiums of £66,000.

Exports
The value of goods exported from the United Kingdom during the year totalled £5.663m. (1979 £2 853m).

Employees
The average number of United Kingdom employees during the year was 1,599 (1979 1,510) and their remuneration totalled £8.847m. (1979 £6.992m.).
The company fully supports the E.E.C. code of conduct for companies with interests in South Africa. A copy of the company policy is available on request from the company secretary.

Donations
During the year the company made a political donation of £1,300 (1979 £1,000) to the Conservative party and charitable donations of £6,000 (1979 £3,000).

Auditors
A resolution to re-appoint Messrs Peat, Marwick, Mitchell & Co will be placed before the annual general meeting on 13th August 1980.

Income and corporation taxes act 1970
The company is not a 'close' company within the meaning of this act.

Inflation accounting
A current cost profit and loss account and balance sheet prepared in accordance with statement of standard accounting practice number 16 are included in the accounts.

Operating subsidiaries and group trading results
see notes 15 and 16, page 25.

Fixed assets
During the year the fixed assets were revalued. The basis of valuation and movements are shown in note 7 page 21. The revaluation surplus of £2.783m. has been transferred to capital reserves.
The revaluation was carried out by Edwards, Bigwood and Bewlay, Surveyors and valuers, Birmingham, and Richard Ellis, Dunlop, Heywood, International real estate economists and brokers, Johannesburg.

By Order of the board
J W Hobbs
Secretary Sandbach
Cheshire CW11 9DN
19th June 1980

Consolidated profit and loss account
for the fifty two weeks ended 29th March 1980

	Note	1980 £000	1979 £000
Sales to external customers		82.126	68.194
Trading profit	1	4,390	3.444
Interest payable on loan capital	2	87	102
Profit before taxation		4.303	3.342
Taxation	3	171	125
Profit after taxation	4	4.132	3.217
Dividends	5	396	275
Retained profit		3,736	2.942
Earnings per ordinary share	6a	56.04p	45.15p
Fully diluted earnings per ordinary share	6b	54.16p	42.52p

Notes to the accounts

7. Fixed assets	Total	Freehold land and buildings	Short-term leasehold buildings	Plant	Office equipment	Motor vehicles
	£000	£000	£000	£000	£000	£000
Cost or valuation at 31st March 1979	5.608	2 499	148	2 526	184	251
Adjustments for currency translations	(4)	(2)	–	(1)	–	(1)
Additions	2.539	1.182	–	955	141	261
Transfer to capital reserve on revaluation	1.299	1.201	(146)	318	(74)	–
	9.442	4.880	2	3.798	251	511
Less disposals	72	–	–	–	1	71
At 29th March 1980						
Cost	1.480	–	2	1.016	22	440
Valuation	7.890	4.880	–	2.782	228	–
	9.370	4.880	2	3.798	250	440

of the accounts will enable you to check further back if necessary. The figure tells you how much the firm made last year from the goods or services it sold to its customers. Company law allows the accounts to leave out this figure if sales – or turnover as its sometimes called – are worth under £5.75 million in most cases.

Profits reveal what's left from the sales income once the firm has paid its normal costs – like raw materials, services the firm has hired, the wage bill, National Insurance, redundancy payments. The biggest single item is usually the wage bill.

The question is: how many 'costs' should the firm knock off before arriving at a fair profit figure? Most companies will claim that the pre-tax profit figure is the fairest one. In other words they treat the directors' pay, the auditors' fees, a notional amount to reflect wear and tear of machinery etc. (depreciation) and interest paid to banks, as extra costs to be docked from the sales income. Many trade unionists disagree. They argue that those costs are no more than a part

45

of the surplus they themselves have helped the firm to create. The correct figure, they say, is the surplus *before* these arbitrary items are subtracted. All the books on company accounts recommended on page 56 have excellent sections on this subject.

In the ERF accounts we've copied, the 'trading profit' figure is the nearest thing to that kind of amount. ERF's £4,390,000 trading profit is their surplus before knocking off interest. But the Notes to the Accounts reveal that they've omitted other sums from that figure: directors' remuneration totalling £147,000, plus depreciation, auditors' fees and other items worth another £1,117,000. But to avoid getting into technical arguments, either figure will at least give you a fair idea of how the firm is doing – even if it doesn't settle the question of how much is in the kitty for the annual wage increase.

Dividends the amount the directors reckon the firm can afford to give the shareholders as a reward for having shares in the company. As the directors are usually shareholders too this is not always the neutral decision it looks. Generally speaking the higher the dividend increase the better the firm is doing.

Interest a key item because it shows how much the company is relying on borrowing. The interest is paid to banks and anyone else the firm has borrowed from. The more the firm is paying out in interest the more it is mortgaging the work-force's jobs.

The *investment* figure is your guide to whether the boss is updating plant, machines and buildings quickly enough to stay competitive. Accountants call these items fixed assets and the additional money spent on them is investment. Again, it's vital to look at more than one year's figures.

What are your companys plans?

Take a look at the following agreement and see if there's anything in it you disagree with:

The Company undertakes to provide Union representatives automatically with the following information:

(1) All information which the Company discloses to its shareholders, loans stockholders or creditors, or to the public.

(2) All decisions by the Company, and all developments specifically relating to the Company, which affect or might affect the employment conditions or prospects of the Union's members, and in particular the following:

(a) Proposed redundancies, short-time working or changes in work methods, organization, materials or equipment.

(b) Proposed closures, rationalization or reorganization schemes.

(c) Proposed changes in product or service lines.

(d) Proposed changes in ownership or control: proposed takeovers or mergers: acquisitions of other companies: changes in senior management.

The chances are that you would like an agreement like this with your own employer. In it, the employer is promising to give the union advance warning of plans that will affect the members. It includes direct-effect plans like redundancies, short-time working, changes in work methods. And there are indirect-effect plans on product and service lines, buying other firms and so on. Take any one of the clauses and decide whether you'd prefer your union to know about the plans before or after they are carried out. And then ask what the set-up is likely to be at your own workplace – has your boss guaranteed you the same kind of protection and willingness to discuss plans? It's a dead cert that the answer is no. So which employer agreed to the clauses weve quoted above?

The answer is none, so far. The clauses are an extract from a model agreement drawn up by the General and Municipal Workers' Union for its shop-stewards. As the union's General Secretary, David Basnett, says:

This movement towards industrial democracy depends, from its earliest stages, on a far greater disclosure of information by employers. Only by this means can workers' representatives begin to evaluate the decisions taken by employers and, if necessary, formulate alternatives.

But the sad fact is that most employers in Britain would not dream of giving workers a fraction of this kind of vital information. Plans are made in British companies with the directors' and shareholders' interests in mind – not the employees'. So we are assuming you have to find out your boss's major plans from other sources.

Getting information on plans   Of the four areas this chapter has looked at – ownership, interests, profits, plans – this is the one where the law and other sources give you least help. Companies' secrecy about their plans is protected by an absence of tough company law and too many toadying financial journalists afraid of rocking the boat. Without the co-operation of your employer – without a good information agreement in other words – there are very few ways you can find out what's in store before the decisions hit you. These are some of the options:

● *The horse's mouth*   The company itself may give away some of its plans in the documents it makes available to the public. Look at the annual report and accounts for a start (see page 53). The subsidiaries your firm has bought, the amount it's investing, exporting or producing abroad, can all be pointers to its plans. The Chairman's Statement is often quite frank about what the firm has in mind for the future. Even if the hints are only broad ones they could be more than you're getting now. If your company is a public one you can buy a share and get all the documents that are sent to the shareholders.

The company should also give you advance warning of *redundancies* it plans – as much as ninety days if a hundred or more jobs are to be chopped. This is a legal requirement – you can get a free guide called 'Redundancy' at your local Employment Offices. In fact, many employers ignore the legal requirements and pay the relatively small penalties involved.

● *The media*   Companies sometimes tell financial journalists and reporters a lot more than they tell their employees. If your shop-stewards' or branch committee can afford it, it's worth subscribing to, say, the *Financial Times*; and checking the *Investors' Chronicle* index once every three months (see page 55). Your local paper or radio station may pick up the occasional 'leak' about your firm's plans too.

● *The union* Remember that your union may have members employed by your boss in other parts of the country. They may know more about what's going on than you do. The union head office may be able to pass on helpful information, or it could put you in touch with other works.

But I don't work for a company

Chapter one showed why the production process in companies gives workers a *right* to be involved in the decisions about their jobs and their work. Our example on page 14 illustrated that no company makes money until its work-force starts producing. It showed that a company's rolling 'snowball' of wealth may be the *combined* result of shareholders' investment and workers' labour – but that it's the shareholders who own both the wealth and the labour. Only their power to bargain with companies gives workers in the private sector any control over what their employers do.

Workers in the public sector are in a different position in one key respect. Their employer, directly or indirectly, is a government that is democratically elected by themselves and the rest of the electorate. In the public sector the equivalent of the private shareholder is the government. So we can say that the way the government finances local authorities, runs the NHS and the nationalized industries, is the way the electorate has authorized. What a company employee produces, as we've said, becomes wealth that is owned by someone else – shareholders – and something that he or she must bargain about to get a share of. But work a hospital worker or a coal miner does is the property of the community, or

49

the public, via their votes for the government that finances the hospital and the mine.

This is certainly not to say that the way the public sector works now is perfect. It is possible to think of other ways in which the community might control much more effectively the industries and services it owns. Many of those ways would give the public sector workers themselves more direct control than just the vote they have in national elections – seats on the council for local government workers is just one example.

What implications does this have for the way we have looked at employers in this chapter? In the first place it means there is no confusion over who your employer is, or what its other activities are. Figure 1 opposite provides a skeleton guide to the shape of the public sector and the services and businesses it owns.

As far as finances and plans are concerned there are several equivalents of company annual accounts in the form of, for example:

- Nationalized Industries' Report and Accounts
- Local Authority Abstract of Accounts
- Health Authority financial plans

But in this area, public sector workers will often face as many problems as company employees in getting information early enough and local enough. Regional Health Authority financial plans, for instance, won't reveal which hospitals are to close even if their money allocation from government guarantees that some must. The RHA will delegate that decision to the next level down, where the District Health Authority (formerly Area Health Authority) decides how to distribute cuts in its own district. By the time a firm proposal is passed on to your local Community Health Council, as closure plans must be, it could be too late to put up effective resistance. As a local government worker you could find your council's accounts abstract as unhelpful as many industrial shop-stewards find their firm's annual report. It could be more valuable to make sure you see the documents and minutes produced by council committees – especially those of any overseeing

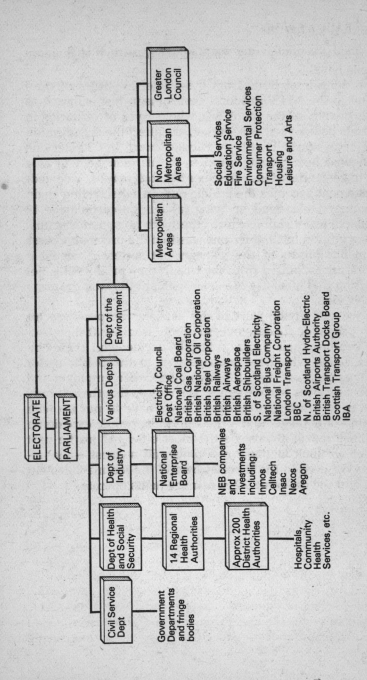

Figure 1 The Shape of the Public Sector

body like the Policy and Resources Committee that many councils have.

One thing is obvious from these brief examples of clue-chasing in the NHS and local government: just as much as in the private sector there is a whole layer of obstacles to penetrate before you, as a worker, can affect the organization that employs you. That layer is *management*. In Chapter one we showed how private business instals management as a lever to get its decisions implemented and, maybe, accepted. Management becomes the middle rank in a *de*scending chain of command – instead of being (as our quote on page 18 suggested) just a skill like any other with no superior status. Our suggestion in Chapter one was that the private business system has produced the management system it needs. If workers are separated from the wealth they produce it is not surprising that business uses management the way the army uses NCOs.

As we said at the start of this section, the public sector doesn't separate its employees entirely from what they produce because their votes indirectly decide who their employer is. So why does management in the public sector appear as the same sort of brick wall between employer and worker as it does in companies? Is it simply that there is only one way to run organizations? Do we have to put up with one kind of management – the kind most people experience – because it will always be the most efficient? In the next chapter we look at these questions and suggest some answers. We explain the theories behind the job management does, and the different ways managements operate.

Where to get the facts you need

The source you want	The facts it will give you	Where you'll find it

Annual Accounts
statement companies must publish every year
	● the firm's finances including profits
	● a *Directors' Report*
	● any subsidiaries
	● name of parent company
	● directors' pay
	● dividends paid to shareholders
		Companies House
		  55–71 City Road,
		London EC1
		  Crown Way, Maindy,
		Cardiff
		  102 George Street,
		Edinburgh
		Direct from your employer if you're lucky

Annual Report 'glossy' version of *Annual Accounts* put out by public companies	● same as *Annual Accounts*. Usual extras are a statement by the chairman, which may include some useful titbits of information ● a record of results over several years ● sometimes more helpful breakdown of subsidiaries and foreign interests	From the company itself. These reports are meant to be freely available, so there's no need to say you're an employee or union official when asking for one
Chairman's Statement preface to most *Annual Reports*	● often just a chance for the chairman of the firm to indulge in a bit of trumpet blowing or heavy hints to government ● occasionally some useful pointers to plans, results and prospects	In the first few pages of the *Annual Report*

The source you want	The facts it will give you	Where you'll find it
Directors' Report		
legally required part of the *Annual Accounts*	● the firm's main activities ● names of the directors ● shares held by directors ● anyone owning 5 per cent or more of the shares ● number of workers employed and total pay bill (larger firms only) ● value of exports ● new subsidiaries or share issues ● political gifts of over £200	Towards the front of the *Annual Accounts*
Directory of Directors		
commercial publication	● names of most company directors ● their directorships	Bigger public libraries
Extel Cards		
commercial service	● financial and other data on public companies going back over several years	Major public libraries Cards on *individual firms* cost £1.65 (public companies), £4.95 (private companies) from Extel, 37/45 Paul Street, London EC2. Phone 01 253 3400
Local Authority Accounts		
equivalent of company accounts – required by law	● a local government version of what you'll get from company *Annual Accounts*	The town hall and often local libraries too, which may also have minutes of council meetings, reports and so on
Nationalized Industry Reports		
required by law	● nationalized industry version of company *Annual Accounts* for Coal Board, British Rail, Post Office, etc	HM Stationery Office Major libraries Direct from the office of the bigger industries

The source you want	The facts it will give you	Where you'll find it
Stock Exchange Yearbook		
commercial publication	● index of all public companies ● plus registered address, and details on shares, subsidiaries and directors	Bigger public libraries
Who Owns Whom?		
commercial publication	● exactly what the title suggests – a cross check of which firms own and belong to which	Bigger public libraries

Some Shortcuts

The source you want	The facts it will give you	Where you'll find it
Your union research department	● will have most of the publications mentioned in this list ● may subscribe to a company information service ● may answer your enquiries direct	Nearly all the bigger unions now have research departments
Labour Research Department		
independent union research group	● LRD run an enquiry service for affiliates. The service includes their reports on any company's accounts and answers to specific queries about firms and directors	78 Blackfriars Road, London SE1
Investors' Chronicle		
commercial weekly publication	● analysis of results of all major firms as they're published	From newsagents; *Company Index* published every three months

The source you want	The facts it will give you	Where you'll find it
Financial Times daily newspaper	● analysis of results of all major firms and nationalized industries as they're published, plus share prices	From newsagents

Note that under recent legislation smaller companies are now exempt from some disclosure provisions – ask your union for details.

Further reading

There are now a number of good and inexpensive guides on the things this chapter has talked about. The ones below are all written from a trade union viewpoint and will take you further into the subject. There's a fair amount of overlap between what the first three cover; the GMWU concentrate on information disclosure claims; while the fifth book takes a case study approach.

Using Company Accounts (Labour Research Department, 1980).

C. Hird *Your Employer's Profits* (Pluto Press, 1975).

M. Barratt Brown *Information at Work* (Arrow, 1978).

Information Disclosure (General and Municipal Workers' Union, 1978).

M. Gold, H. Levie and R. Moore *The Shop Steward's Guide to the Use of Company Information* (Spokesman Books, 1979).

Chapter **Three**

How does management manage?

As Britain's recession deepened throughout 1980/81 the cry went up that Britain's workers were slowly coming round to recognizing 'new economic realities'. It was said, particularly by the 'popular' press, that at last workers were rejecting shop-floor militancy, accepting 'sensible' wage increases, and recognizing management's right to manage. What the recession certainly did was to force workers on to the defensive. Real fears for jobs and a sense that government policy was designed to reduce workers' living standards and the effectiveness of their trade unions, combined to create a mood of demoralization which employers were quick to exploit.

Take a look at the comments below of two industrialists at the end of 1980 which illustrate management's new assertiveness:

Managers for twenty years have had a buffeting and bashing from governments and unions and have been put into a 'can't win' situation . . . We have an opportunity now that will last for two or three years. Then, the unions will get themselves together again . . . One of the tasks right now is to persuade senior managers to persuade middle managers to get up and run. There is no lack of know-how. It's a matter of seeing what opportunities there are. We have had a pounding and we are all fed up with it. I think it would be fair to say that it's almost vengeance.

(Len Collinson, director of Wormald International Holdings)

'It is absolutely unacceptable to manage through the unions. I do ask their advice, but not whether I can do something or not. Management is paid to take the decisions . . . The man on the shop-floor knows what he is required to do. It is a question of expect and inspect. When the foreman has told a man what is expected, we start inspecting.'

(Andy Barr, plant director, BL Longbridge)

What the present economic climate has done is to bring into sharp focus certain common management attitudes. This chapter draws out and explains some of the attitudes and approaches which lie behind management practice today. It tries to show what management is all about.

What makes management tick?

We are going to answer this question by looking at how the *practice* of management has developed. Although it's a common temptation for trade unionists to write-off this kind of discussion, we think that that attitude is mistaken. This chapter contains a strong plea for knowing more about what motivates management so that a more effective trade union response can be created to the forms that management power and authority take at the place of work. Just as no trade unionist should feel properly equipped to respond to a health or safety hazard without first fully understanding what constitutes the hazard, so no trade unionist should feel properly equipped to respond to a management initiative without knowing the objectives which hide behind the initiative.

This chapter concentrates on the broad questions underlining the role and objectives of management. It is not our purpose to look at various management techniques in detail (such as work study or job evaluation). Our aim is no more, and no less, than to identify those considerations which underpin every facet of management decision-making. But is this relevant to the *public sector*? While it might appear that much of what we're going to say will be relevant only to those employed in the private sector, we would argue strongly that management practice in the public sector is founded on the same assumptions, attitudes and objectives commonly found in private enterprise.

In this first section we ask the question: what is the role of profit in management decision-making? Profit makes every enterprise tick. Making profits – and the bigger the profits the better – is the common objective of modern capitalist industry.

In very simple terms profit results from the following sequence of events: First, the businessman starts with a sum of money which he will use to produce goods or services for sale. He uses raw materials, labour and machinery in this process. Labour operates the machinery which transforms the raw materials into goods for sale. The additional money the businessman gets from the sale of these goods is his *profit*.

If, therefore, that same businessman can:

- keep the price of his raw materials low;
- keep his wage costs down;
- keep his machinery operating continuously and efficiently;
- keep up the price of the goods he sells;

then he makes more profit.

In all capitalist enterprises management's role is to ensure that profit targets are met. One of America's leading writers on management theory referred to this as 'the first function' of management:

Management must always, in every decision and action, put economic performance first. It can only justify its existence and its authority by the economic results it produces. There may be great non-economic results . . . Yet management has failed if it does not supply goods and services desired by the consumer at a price the consumer is willing to pay. It has failed if it does not improve, or at least maintain, the wealth-producing capacity of the economic resources entrusted to it.

In sharper language he added that if the original decision to go into business was sound then it was the responsibility of management to make the business produce the needed minimum profit, 'that, bluntly, is what managements are being paid for'.

Two key roles for management

How then does management meet the objective of making profits? To do this management has two main tasks.

Firstly, management must coordinate the various activities of the enterprise. This is done by planning the use of available resources and organizing the way in which resources are deployed. It means, for example, that the right materials are in the right place at the right time. It means as well that finance must be made available for the purchase of raw materials and tools and the payment of wages. This requirement is common to all forms of economic organization, not just capitalist enterprises.

Secondly, management 'manages' workers and work. This means telling people what to do and seeing that they do it.

It is this latter role – of managing workers and work – which marks out management in capitalist society and is the main focus of this chapter.

Managing workers and work

Management has always searched for better ways of managing workers and work. With the rise of modern capitalism in the nineteenth century and the factory system's need for work discipline, management became a more clearly defined, better organized and more scientific activity. There developed various theories of how best to manage firms based on some form of scientific method. In the 1880s and 1890s for example, the major thrust was on piece-work payment systems. But the term 'scientific management' is generally associated with the ideas of F. W. Taylor, whose book *The Principles of Scientific Management* appeared in 1899.

Scientific management

The core of scientific management was the organized study of work, the analysis of work into its simplest elements and the systematic improvement of the workers' performance of each of these elements.

Taylor distinguished between what he called *ordinary* management and *scientific* management. Through ordinary management, according to Taylor, managers tried to encourage 'each workman to use his best endeavours, his hardest work, all his traditional knowledge, his skill, his ingenuity and his goodwill – in a word, his "initiative", so as to yield the largest possible return to his employer'. Thus in a very crude sense the relationship between management and workers depended on notions of trust and cooperation.

In contrast, scientific management allowed managers greater control over the process of production by controlling *all* decisions at work. In other words whereas 'trust' was all very well, 'control' was better. For Taylor the basic principles of scientific management were:

● Specifying and timing all work tasks in absolute detail.
● Removing all 'brain work' from the shop-floor and locating it in central planning departments.
● Taking away all initiative from individual workers and replacing individual initiative by work systems to which all workers conformed.

This was the essence of what became know as 'Taylorism', with time-and-motion study soon emerging as a central element in its application to industry.

Weaknesses of Taylorism

After the First World War, firms in America and Britain began to introduce time-and-motion study and determine work tasks based on these studies. But there were two big problems with Taylorism. The first was the assumption that because work can be analysed into its simplest constituent motions it should also be *organized* as a series of individual motions, each preferably carried out by a separate worker. But it was not the case then, and is not the case now, that the simpler the motion or operation, the better the worker will perform it. It is in the nature of a worker's intelligence that he or she will always wish to perform many 'motions' – 'to integrate, to balance, to control, to measure, to judge' – and not be confined to a single operation.

The second problem with Taylorism was that it separated 'planning' from 'doing'. 'Planning' quite correctly was identified as a separate part of a job, but Taylor's mistake was to insist that the 'planner' and the 'doer' should be two separate people. He could not see that 'planning' and 'doing' were legitimately separate parts of the *same* job.

Taylorism meant *workers were denied direct control over their work*, with initiative and self-pacing replaced by boredom and monotony. Somehow, therefore, workers had to be compensated. To persuade workers to accept Taylorism, firms offered higher wages. But once these new techniques were firmly established, management began to cut wage rates (or piece-rates). The system was being seen as too crude and unsophisticated, and workers and their unions were beginning to 'work' it. By the late 1920s Taylorism was coming under serious attack from managers. One critic said the system would only survive where immigrant labour was cheap and trade unions weak. Other critics emphasized that its application always increased workers resistance to further innovation and change in working methods:

Because he is being taught individual motions rather than given a job, his ability to unlearn is stifled rather than developed. He acquires experience and habit rather than knowledge and understanding. Because the worker is supposed to do rather than to know – let alone to plan – every change represents the challenge of the incomprehensible and therefore threatens his psychological security.

Peter Drucker *The Practice of Management* (Pan Books, 1968)

By the late 1930s, Taylorism had fallen into general disfavour and more sophisticated approaches were being looked for.

Although Taylorism as a total system may have disappeared into the annals of history its influence has continued to remain strong especially on work methods and production techniques (for example, in work simplification, tool and machine engineering, and production control processes).

Indeed at the same time as scientific management was introduced, flow production made its appearance (for a present day example of what flow production means for workers, see the 'Riverside' example, p. 79). Because flow production meant management control over the speed of production lines it very much complemented Taylorism. It had been introduced in the United States by Henry Ford before the First World War and in the 1920s and 1930s was having a big impact in British industry. For managers flow production had the advantage of replacing human supervision by the supervision of the line. Thus, in theory at least, a cocktail of Taylorism and line speed-ups brought new possibilities for increasing profits.

The human relations movement

But, for managers, what were the alternatives to Taylorism? From the late 1920s a new school of so-called management science made its appearance – the 'human relations movement'. Broadly speaking the movement accepted scientific management's objectives of efficiency (greater profitability) by control, but focused on individuals and small group processes rather than large organizations, emphasizing 'communication', 'leadership', and 'interpersonal relations'. The movement's leading advocates were a new breed of 'scientists' who styled themselves industrial psychologists (developing systems of performance rating, together with techniques for measuring and improving employee morale), industrial sociologists (analysing enterprises as social systems), applied anthropologists (studying forms of human organization), and social psychologists (studying, for example, techniques of propaganda).

Their practical proposals have involved:

- 'Making work more interesting', 'making work more human' (see pages 85–7).
- Choosing workers who would best fit the job requirements.
- Encouraging a sense of 'team spirit' and identification with the enterprise. By offering workers status, authority and responsibility management would try to win their loyalty to the firm's ideals. It sometimes meant getting the trade union to closely identify itself with the interests of the firm. Currently much enthusiasm is being expressed for the role that 'quality circles' may have in improving worker motivation, productivity and quality. Their key characteristics are as follows: small groups of about ten people meet on a voluntary but regular basis to discuss their workplace problems (organization, quality or whatever it happens to be). They usually meet for about an hour once every week or fortnight, and by means of problem-solving techniques, they analyse the difficulties they see as most relevant and acute. They recommend solutions to management, whenever possible implementing them themselves. The circle leader is usually the supervisor or foreman of the work area involved.

One of the most influential expressions of the human relations approach came from Peter Drucker in his *Practice of Management*, published in 1955. One chapter – 'Human Organization for Peak Performance' – constituted what Drucker called his 'manifesto'. He argued that by proclaiming 'peak performance' to be the goal, management had to consider more than human relations. Yet by stressing human organization, it was necessary to go beyond traditional scientific management. A blending of the two approaches was necessary therefore.

The first requirement was the engineering of the individual job for maximum efficiency. This could be done by:

- Applying scientific management to the analysis and organization of work.
- Improving performance of the individual motions or parts of the job.
- Laying out systematically and according to the logical flow of the work the various motions to be performed.
- Putting the parts or motions of the job into an integral whole.

The second requirement was to organize people to do the work in a way which would serve the best interests of the enterprise. Workers would have to be motivated before peak performance could be obtained and it was maintained that this could only be done by giving workers responsibility. In Drucker's view there were four ways of reaching the objective of the 'responsible worker' by:

- Putting the worker on the job he or she will do best.
- Achieving high standards of performance through high job demands.
- Providing the worker with the information he or she needed to measure and guide his or her own performance.
- Giving the worker a 'managerial vision', in other words seeing the enterprise as if he or she were a manager responsible, through his or her performance, for its success.

All these ideas are about creating systems of work where workers *believe* they are doing jobs which reflect their interests and skills. The reality of course is different. It is no more than an alternative strategy for management to impose its control over workers.

Since the late 1950s the approach of the human relations movement has experienced certain revisions. Basically these have been changes of style and presentation rather than of substance. Management theory has become increasingly dependent on sophisticated research methods and investigations, but the objective remains the same – to achieve for management practice the most effective means of coordinating the economic activities of the enterprise and of controlling work and workers.

How are you controlled?

So far we have argued that two objectives are common to the management of capitalist enterprises – the coordination of economic activities and the control of work and workers. Our particular focus on the latter continues in this section by considering the ways in which control is enforced. But before we do that one qualification needs to be made.

Whereas managements share this common objective there may be major differences between enterprises in the way management seeks to achieve it. Management will determine its general approach on the basis of a whole range of factors. Crude Taylorism, because it erodes the quality of working life, is less likely to be applied where trade union organization is effective and the bargaining power of the work-group strong. Equally where management is hard-nosed and convinced it has a god-given right to manage unrestrained by any trade union presence, there will not be much sympathy for 'making work more human'.

These considerations will be reflected for example in the way enterprises deal with labour questions. Even within a single company separate plants may be subject to different approaches. In Vickers, at their Slingsby plant in Yorkshire, producing fibreglass mini-submarines, gliders and naval furniture, management on a number of occasions has escorted union representatives off the site and refused permission for shop meetings because 'they don't consider them necessary'. At the same time at KTM Brighton, machine-tool manufacturers and again part of the Vickers combine, management acceded to the shop-stewards committee having a full-time convenor with an office and telephone extension.

Let's return now to the purpose of this section – to examine ways in which control is enforced. We do this by looking at the use management makes of *status*, *discipline* and *mechanization*, three issues central to the balance of power at work.

Everyone in their place

In workplaces where employees are divided between those who are hourly-paid and those on staff status it's a common question to ask why staff, including managers, should get non-wage or 'fringe' benefits, such as access to the company pension scheme or private medical treatment, which are denied to the hourly-paid. This section then asks: Why is it that the employees of an enterprise are treated differently according to their *status* in the enterprise?

In a modern capitalist economy virtually all forms of corporate organization – in both private and public sectors – are characterized by what we call hierarchical control. Look at Figure 2, which illustrates a fairly typical large company structure. Note how top management exercises overall control. The directors of the company are there to ensure that the company meets its profits targets each year, while each level of management below the top board is responsible directly or indirectly for meeting these objectives. Figure 3 shows how this is achieved. Note how the responsibilities of each level of management are defined from the top. Note also how each level of management is accountable to the level above for providing a constant flow of information so that at the very top the directors know how successful the company is at achieving the profit targets which have been set.

Within each unit of the organization each job will be rigidly defined according to:

- the work done;
- the power and responsibility that goes with it;
- the status it carries in the organization.

Each job again fits into a finely graded structure (a bit like a pyramid) and workers at each level of the structure are responsible to, and controlled by, those in the level above.

We can illustrate this by looking at a fairly typical modern factory organization. Look at Figure 4. At the bottom level are production line workers, skilled craftsmen and all those involved in constructing, creating and assembling. In short, all those who either directly, or through tools and machinery, work the raw materials into the finished product.

At the level above, supervising and controlling their work, are foremen and first line supervisors.

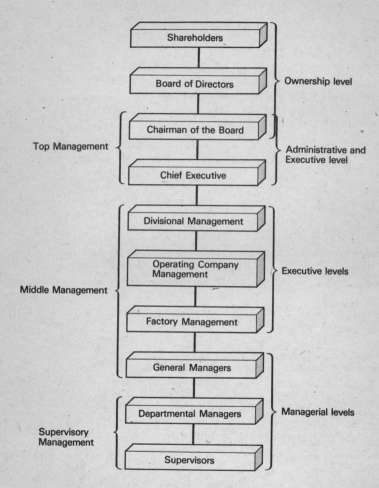

Figure 2 A typical Company Structure

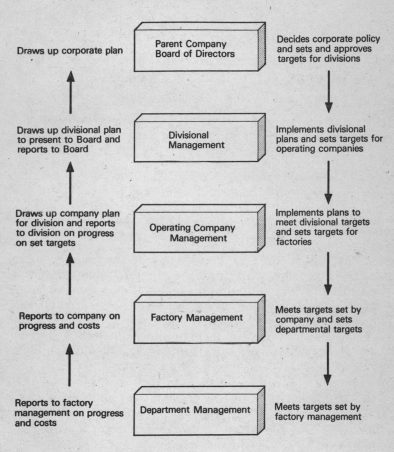

Draws up corporate plan	**Parent Company Board of Directors**	Decides corporate policy and sets and approves targets for divisions
Draws up divisional plan to present to Board and reports to Board	**Divisional Management**	Implements divisional plans and sets targets for operating companies
Draws up company plan for division and reports to division on progress on set targets	**Operating Company Management**	Implements plans to meet divisional targets and sets targets for factories
Reports to company on progress and costs	**Factory Management**	Meets targets set by company and sets departmental targets
Reports to factory management on progress and costs	**Department Management**	Meets targets set by factory management

Figure 3 Management Control

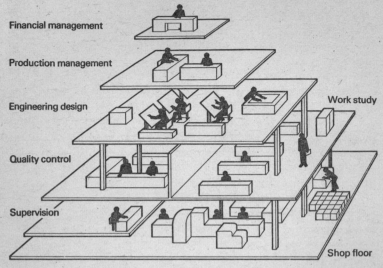

Financial management

Production management

Engineering design

Work study

Quality control

Supervision

Shop floor

Figure 4 Hierarchical structure in a typical modern factory organization

Industrial Democracy, BBC, 1976

Above this are the lower levels of production management, quality control and work study, who in turn are directed and controlled by succeeding higher levels of management.

At the very top all are subject to the authority of the managing director or whoever exercises executive power on behalf of the owners of the enterprise, in the pursuit of whose interests the whole structure is created and continues to function.

You will notice that throughout the structure there is a clear separation of those who make the decisions from those who carry them out. At any one level (except the bottom) decisions are made which are carried out at the level below. Indeed at each level in the hierarchy, except at the very bottom and at the very top, individuals will be on the taking end and receiving end of the decision-making process. The higher up you are in the structure, the bigger the influence you have over the decision-making process and the greater your rewards.

The system necessarily implies that tight control over all areas of work is built into the structure. This means that the system removes discretion and control over work from the hands of workers.

But don't assume that managers are free agents. They're caught up in the system as well. At managerial levels loyalty to the firm is enforced by an extended promotion system in which the only way to improve your position is to adopt all the ideals, values and strategy of the firm as your own.

Take supervisors, for example. The supervisor's role involves a mixture of responsibilities from planning and scheduling work so that it flows evenly, ensuring adequate provision of equipment and materials, to establishing objectives for workers and enforcing discipline. The nature of these tasks has usually encouraged top management to recruit supervisors from the shop-floor, but the supervisor's job is very much a management job, attracting management status. Yet, as elsewhere in the hierarchy, supervisors are 'subordinates' as well as 'superiors', for while they exercise control over workers, they in turn are subject to the control of top management. Job engineering, work organization, the workers' economic relationship to the enterprise, and the structure and practice of the enterprise are not determined by the supervisor – but by top management.

So far we have concentrated our attention on capitalist enterprises, but is there any relevance in what we have had to say for the public sector, be it nationalized industries or public services? The following case study on hierarchical control in the National Health Service suggests that the public-owned sector constitutes a mirror image of practices common to capitalist enterprises.

Hierarchical control: a case study – the NHS The creation of a National Health Service in 1948 reflected the popular demand that health care should come under public ownership to allow:

● fairer access to health care (based on need and not ability to pay);

- fairer distribution of health care resources (between rich and poor areas for example);
- a more socially equitable system of health care provision.

But as a recent booklet by Daniel Vulliamy and Roger Moore has shown ('Whitleyism and Health', WEA, 1979) there were other powerful reasons supporting the establishment of the National Health Service. It was expected that:

- centralized control would minimize costs;
- a healthier work-force would be a more productive work-force;
- the costs of health care would progressively fall, as an increasingly healthy work-force would be less prone to illness.

Politicians, civil servants and administrators within the service have consistently supported these arguments since 1948. The result is that the NHS has developed management practices little different to those common in capitalist enterprises.

There was major reorganization of management and methods in the NHS between the mid-1950s and mid-1970s. The first phase saw modern management methods introduced at all levels. In place of general administrators, specialist officers were created, particularly in ancillary areas like catering, laundries, supplies and purchasing. Management services were streamlined and rose in both size and status. This was especially true of work study, organizational methods, training and personnel. Furthermore the service began recruiting managers with experience in private enterprise.

The second phase of management change saw the deliberate creation of structured hierarchies in most occupational areas of the service. This process was perhaps clearest in changes in nursing management following publication of the government's Salmon Report in 1966. The Report recommended a separate specialist nurse-management function, dividing clinical work from its management. It meant for example, that matrons were to lose control of non-nursing functions (catering, cleaning, linen, laundry, etc.) to specialist managers. The Report stressed that the skills needed for nursing management were different from those needed for nursing:

Nurses in top management need, most of all, well developed managerial skills. . . Provided he or she has shown the proper managerial ability it does not matter the route taken to the top.

Thinking was clear: nursing management needed strengthening and this would be done best by applying professional management techniques. So a strategy was developed to make senior nurses think like managers and *not* nurses.

In the past, much work now classified as ancillary was performed by nurses (most obviously those tasks now done by domestics and laundry workers). As these tasks have become separated from nursing duties they have tended to become organized on *economic* rather than medical criteria. Thus two Prices and Incomes Reports (1967 and 1971) concluded that the low pay of ancillary workers was linked to their alleged poor productivity which was the result of poor labour-management structures and standards. Both Reports recognized the far-reaching implications for management style and structure of any attempt to relate earnings to effort more directly.

Various criticisms were made of existing management structures. For example, it was said that existing financial control only encouraged keeping within budgets and was not concerned with reducing costs. The Reports called for a clear allocation of management responsibilities, the separation of ancillary work from nursing control, tighter job definitions, greater standardization of work methods and equipment, and more centralization of production into fewer units by reducing the total number of hospitals.

These managerial approaches were imported from private industry and assumed a similarity between the *public* control of health care and the *private* control of industry. As a direct consequence management of the NHS has become very much tougher, indeed often more so than in private industry.

Similar changes have occurred elsewhere in the public sector, most notably in local government, where the last major reorganization was introduced at the same time and with the same intentions as the 1974 NHS reorganization.

For public sector workers this raises the issue of whether their state-appointed controllers are in any way different from the controllers of private enterprises. It might be said that the public controllers are accountable to the general public through public ownership. But the real answer seems to be that as public controllers behave more and more like private owners the differences between private industry and the public sector become increasingly marginal.

Cracking the whip

The threat of the sack remains management's ultimate weapon for controlling workers. An employer's right to discipline or ultimately dismiss his employees is sanctioned in law, limited only by unfair dismissal legislation (a useful easy-to-read guide on dismissal law is 'Unfair Dismissal', LRD, 1980). In this section we ask the question: How is discipline used as a means of management control?

We concentrate on the relationship between discipline and profit and begin by looking at an example of the practical application of this relationship.

The Ford case   In the summer of 1980 the Ford Motor Company faced severe financial difficulties. The slump in US car and commercial vehicle sales meant Ford declaring their biggest-ever corporate quarterly loss – $595 million for the third quarter of 1980. For the end of 1980 the company was forecasting a loss of $2 billion against a profit of $1.2 billion in 1979. Ford's US market share, once 30 per cent, had fallen from 23 per cent in 1978 to 17 per cent, and was still falling. In Germany, the biggest market in Europe, the decline had been from 13 per cent to under 10 per cent in less than a year. In the UK, Ford's profits for the second half of 1980 looked as though they were drying up.

Thus the full implications of Ford's losses worldwide were bearing down on the company's closely interlinked European and British management. In these circumstances the successful launch of the new Escort in 1980 took on added significance for the future of Ford's UK operations.

In the summer the new Escort production line had become operational at the Halewood plant on Merseyside. But the new equipment threw up major problems, particularly over safety and manning levels. The general approach of management had been to force the pace – insisting workers operate in certain defined ways, telling them that any consequent problems could be sorted out later. Management's approach led to a number of disputes particularly in the body plant with the constant pressures of tight job times on production lines.

In a clear attempt to raise production levels, particularly at Halewood, Ford UK announced in November 1980 the introduction of a new disciplinary code for all its UK plants. There had been no discussions with the unions. The decision had been taken at the highest European management level within the context of restoring Ford's profitability.

The new code involved the suspension without pay of workers who failed to work normally. They were to be suspended for the remainder of the shift they were working and for the whole of the next one as well. The first application of the new code came at the end of November 1980, at Halewood, in the press shop which had been most affected by changes in work practices brought about by the introduction of the new line. Management said that twenty-two workers, who fed a semi-automatic metal-stamping line, had consistently failed to meet hourly production targets. The men had insisted on following their usual practice of deciding themselves to rotate jobs within their group and when a foreman ordered them to revert to their original work stations they refused and were suspended.

Under the old disciplinary code the men would have been suspended without pay for the rest of that shift, but under the new code the twenty-two were suspended for the next shift as well. 350 fellow night-shift press shop workers stopped work in sympathy and were similarly suspended. By the following morning 2400 workers had been laid off and Escort production brought to a standstill.

The introduction of the new code coincided with the annual national pay negotiations for the 57,000 manual workers in which the unions had submitted a claim for increases of 20 per cent, plus a shorter working week and improved holiday entitlement. Management had responded with a first offer of 7.5 per cent, and a 'final' offer of 9.5 per cent, both of which were rejected by the unions. Significantly, management were making it clear that they were not willing to go further unless the unions entered into firm commitments on working practices, the issue behind the new disciplinary code. Thus for sacrificing elements of the little control that workers exercised over the work process, management offered the possibility of more money in the pocket. The terms of the trade-off were such that which ever choice was made, only management could win.

What should workers do about discipline? In 1977 the Advisory, Conciliation and Arbitration Service (ACAS) issued a Code of Practice entitled 'Disciplinary Practice and Procedures'. This is what it had to say about determining discipline policies:

'Management is responsible for maintaining discipline within the organization and for ensuring that there are adequate disciplinary rules and procedures. The initiative for establishing these will normally be with management. However, if they are to be fully effective the rules and procedures need to be accepted as reasonable both by those who are to be covered by them and by those who operate them.' (our emphasis)

The traditional managerial approach to discipline, perhaps best characterized by the foreman with the power to hire and fire almost at will, favoured harsh penalties geared to detering workers from committing any breach of rules. Since 1972 and the Contracts of Employment Act there is evidence to suggest that management has tended to prefer a more 'enlightened' approach to discipline. This approach has assumed that workers generally are willing to abide by 'well-established, equitable standards of behaviour' and consequently has seen discipline 'largely in terms of fostering self-discipline amongst employees'. It has led to a growing preoccupation among trade unionists with 'getting the procedure right' at the expense of a fundamental questioning of the role discipline serves as a means of controlling work and workers.

Let's look again at the ACAS Code of Practice. It justifies disciplinary rules and procedures for the following reasons:

Disciplinary rules and procedures are necessary for promoting fairness and *order* in the treatment of individuals and in the conduct of industrial relations. They also assist an organization to *operate effectively*. Rules set standards of conduct at work; procedure helps to ensure that the standards are adhered to and also provides a fair method of dealing with alleged failures to observe them. (our emphasis)

Here is clear recognition that disciplinary rules and procedures are essential for the maintenance of 'order' and 'efficiency' (and consequently, profitability). Furthermore, it is the ACAS view (see the first extract from ACAS' code) that workers' acceptance of disciplinary rules and procedures will be dependent largely upon the extent of their involvement in determining them. This poses some big problems for trade unionists.

Experience suggests that what constitutes a disciplinary issue will depend largely on what management choose to call a disciplinary issue. This in turn is dependent on the issues over which management want to exercise control and on the way disciplinary rules are used to control workers' behaviour. Whether workers allow an issue to be treated as an individual disciplinary question, or respond *collectively* becomes very much dependent on the strength of their trade union organization. At any one moment in time this may well depend on a wide range of economic factors.

Casual working in the docks industry did not end until the late 1960s. Up until then it was common for the combination of casual working, the gang system and piece-work, together with the dockers traditional collective bargaining strength, to allow many aspects of work control to be exercised by the men themselves. It was very much a system of the gangs being given the jobs and deciding themselves how and at what speed to do them. It meant especially that workers had control of absenteeism and timekeeping. One working method, known as the 'hop system', allowed shipworkers to take time off and be covered by their informal rota systems for deciding whose day off it was. Another working method, the 'job and finish system', was built around workers easing off in the early afternoon to force the employer to order overtime. With the order given, and, for example, a two-hour period paid for, the job would be completed and workers would go home, invariably before the two-hour period had been worked.

These two examples show how certain elements of work control were denied to management and how workers assumed the responsibility for controlling the work activities, including behaviour, of their colleagues. In such a situation management could not control absenteeism or timekeeping practices by relying on formal rules. If any change was desired management would have had to negotiate new manning levels collectively with the men.

This suggests that if your trade union organization is strong you may well be able to do without formal disciplinary procedures. You may be able to rely on either sorting out any problems you have on an informal basis or by using the disputes and grievance procedure to process disciplinary cases. But if you are less confident of your trade union organization then disciplinary procedures may well have to be agreed with management to protect workers against unfair disciplinary action. The TUC has usefully suggested that a disciplinary procedure should make sure that:

● Where industrial misconduct is alleged the worker is given *warning* and an *opportunity to improve*.
● A worker's immediate supervisor doesn't have the authority to dismiss him or her.
● At all stages in the procedure the worker has the *right to be represented* by a trade union representative.
● Any worker subject to disciplinary action can *appeal* on all decisions.

● Trade union representatives are not disciplined without reference to the union.

An end to skills?

We have seen that it is a management objective to allow workers as little real control as possible over the organization of their work. This approach is reinforced by management seeking to define every detail of work and mechanize jobs.

Of course, the two are inter-related and the final result is to reduce steadily the skill and imagination that workers use in performing their work. The question we ask in this section is therefore: how does management use technological change to tighten its control over work and workers?

With the mass of workers performing ever more simple and mundane tasks and with processes becoming more automated and complex, workers lose whatever control they may have had over the work process. Not only does job content become machine-determined, but management decides the pace at which tasks are performed. In the example which follows – 'ChemCo' – we see a practical illustration of this.

Huw Beynon and Theo Nichols have described how management's use of technological change has affected workers lives at a fertilizer plant in the north of England. 'Riverside' is a technologically advanced chemical complex, yet despite this most of the men employed as manual workers perform heavy, repetitive, boring work.

Here, and at 'ChemCo' generally, it is clear that the new (scientific) skills associated with advanced chemical production are not concentrated on the factory floor, rather in the hands of the controllers. . .

At Riverside a conveyor belt has removed the need for trotting – a definite technological advance. But only to ensure that more fertilizer is packed. . . At peak rates Zap and Zap X are packed at sixty tons an hour, one ton a minute, a hundredweight bag every three seconds.

The packer stands under the hopper spout at the end of the packing band. He takes a plastic bag off the top of the pile which stands to his right, shakes it open and holds it under the spout. A swift upward motion releases a measured hundredweight into the bag and on to the rollers. All in three seconds. . . The full bags are sealed by pulling the open end taut, folding it over and feeding it through a heated slot that automatically closes the bag. From here they roll to the loading bay where, at the 'band end', they thud on to the shoulders of the two loaders. If the bags are going 'to road', the two men stack them three or five deep on to the back of a lorry. They catch the bags, turn and drop them. Catch, turn, drop . . . catch, turn, drop. . . Every *six* seconds.

Huw Beynon and Theo Nichols, *Living with Capitalism*, 1977

In this example technology allowed management to control the pace of work, but there are many other ways in which the application of technology allows management to extend its control over the work process.

Mechanization has been a continuous process throughout history and there can be little doubt that micro-electronic technology, the 'new technology', will have results as far-reaching for workers as any period of technological innova-tion in the past. The impact of new technology on jobs is well documented and some of the political as well as econ-omic questions this raises for trade unionists are taken up in Chapter six. In this section we concentrate on the implica-tions of new technology for management control at work.

In other words the introduction of new technology allows management increased control of who does what, when and how. It means for workers a reduction in skill, status and job security. If these appear sweeping statements they are made because consequences for workers *are* so profound. This is how one recent study has summed up the situation:

The potential of systems of work based on microprocessor technol-ogy for shifting the distribution of knowledge within the firm is so great that we may be at a watershed. Traditionally, workers had to have a certain amount of technical knowledge and an awareness of where work fitted into the general economy, simply so that the whole system of practices could hang together. Despite the attempts of work study and automation this is still substantially the case in many areas of work today. Micro-electronic technology promises to alter that radically, and soon.

Why is this so? If workers understand how a job is done, if their skill and experience are essential elements of the job, then they have some control over it. But when a machine incorporates the skills previously employed by workers their control disappears because management can use that machine to control all aspects of the work process including the speed and intensity of work. To see how this happens we're going to look at how the introduction of new technology in general and word processors in particular has affected office work.

Word processors and control at work – a case study It's said that more workers are employed in offices in the industrialized world than in any other type of work. In the UK 45 per cent of the total work-force are clerical and administrative workers. The application of Taylorism during the early decades of this century, with its emphasis on separating 'planning' from 'doing' (see page 62), began the massive growth of workers employed in the acquisition, storage, transfer and presentation of information which constitutes 'office work' to this day. Whereas microprocessors have an enormous range of applications throughout the economy, it's in the office that their application has the advantage of dealing directly with the thing they are designed to process – information. The current range of microprocessor-based office equipment includes:

● small business computers;
● optical character recognition equipment;
● computer-controlled telephone exchanges and switching systems;
● facsimile transmitters;
● mass electronic storage devices;
● word processors.;

The comprehensive application of this kind of technology could massacre office jobs. Siemens Co.'s notorious 'Office 1990' report for example estimated that 40 per cent of all clerical-type jobs could be standardized and that 25–30 per cent could then be fully automated. But while not under-

81

estimating the impact on job loss, it's the implications for management control which concern us here. By looking at just one element of the available hardware – word processors – we'll draw out some of these implications.

Essentially word processors are 'intelligent' typewriters. Like many other forms of new technology they *could* contribute to an improvement in the quality of working life. But they pose a threat to workers because management seeks their introduction as a way of further controlling work. Word processors are based on micro-electronic technology and offer a large number of different facilities to increase the productivity of typing operations. A typical word processor consists of a keyboard, a visual display unit (VDU), a printer and some form of storage capacity (usually magnetic discs), plus a central processing unit which gives the system 'intelligence'. The productivity of word processing technology, in terms of letters or documents produced, is estimated at between 100 and 300 per cent above traditional methods of production. The word processor reduces the time that is necessary to produce a document by eliminating retyping (through self-correction) and reduces the labour that is needed – work previously requiring three typists can now be done by one operator. Not surprisingly the current annual growth rate in sales of word processing systems is 40 per cent.

How then does the word processor increase managerial control? Firstly, the standardized operation of word processors reduces the individual worker's ability to apply his or her particular skills to the job. Secondly, word processors are likely to depersonalize working relationships within the office as the provision of overall typing services replaces individual secretary-manager relationships. Thirdly, as work tasks become more rigidly defined with non-typing functions, such as filing, telephoning, being removed from the word processor operator, so work becomes further fragmented. Fourthly, the ability of the word processor to 'memorize' a worker's output allows new possibilities for monitoring work. Finally, hierarchical control is enhanced as the top administrative and secretarial jobs of the few get further separated from the routine machine-minding of the many. A report published by the International Labour Organization commented that 'because the microprocessor makes communication and the provision of information so easy, so quick and so cheap, it also makes it possible to centralize control'.

Strangers bearing gifts – management-initiated change

We said at the beginning of this chapter that it was important for trade unionists to be clear in their minds why management operates the way it does. This is especially important when trade unionists are required to respond to management initiated changes in work organization and decision-making. In this section we look at changes which management has initiated which seem to increase workers' relative control over their work. We argue that these can often be used as a screen to reduce the effectiveness of trade union organization in the workplace. We ask two questions therefore: Can any real changes be made at work which do not threaten management's 'right to manage'? Have changes in work practices, which management claimed would lessen supervision, led to any weakening of management control?

Below we take two examples of how management has sought to maintain its control over work and workers by drawing workers into the decision-making process without releasing control. By getting workers and unions to accept responsibility for decisions which remain firmly management's prerogative trade union aims become confused and trade union workplace organization weakened. The two examples are the British Steel Corporation's worker director scheme and Volvo's so-called 'humanization of work' experiments.

British Steel Corporation Following the nationalization of the industry in 1967, the Organizing Committee of BSC proposed to the TUC that employee directors be introduced in the Corporation as a means of developing the collective bargaining and joint consultation procedures of the industry.

An agreed limited scheme emerged but with no precise definition of the role employee directors were to play.

It was agreed that:

- Up to three employee directors would be appointed to each Group Board.
- Appointees would work at their normal jobs when not undertaking their director role.
- The appointments would be made by the Chairman of the Corporation from a short list of names provided by the TUC from employees of BSC.
- Part-time trade union officers could be appointed but *they would be expected to resign their trade union positions*.
- Employee directors would serve on the Group Boards responsible for the works in which they were employed.
- The employee directors would be appointed for three years and would receive a salary of £1000 per annum, plus compensation for any loss of normal earnings.
- The scheme was to be regarded as experimental and reviewed in consultation with the TUC.

With clear lines of accountability to the trade union movement broken, and having been appointed and not elected, the first twelve employee directors began work in March 1968. As a result of structural changes within the Corporation, which replaced the Group Boards with Product Divisions, four further employee directors were appointed in 1970 (with the total number finally increased to seventeen in 1974).

By 1971 it had become clear that the scheme showed particular weaknesses in the relationship of the employee directors to the trade unions. In the hope of correcting the situation the following amendments to the scheme were suggested and made effective by April 1973:

- Employee directors should be able to hold any *part-time* union office.
- Employee directors should be invited to attend joint consultative meetings between unions and management, and be encouraged to participate in advisory committees and working parties at appropriate levels within the Corporation.

● The selection process should be amended to allow greater participation of employees and their representatives.

But despite these changes the system continued to show major weaknesses. In a damning indictment a major research study in 1976 concluded that:

The worker directors had no effect on the decision-making process because the Board was not really where it occurred. Even if it had been, things would have changed little, management have a monopoly of knowledge, of language; *the worker directors were individuals with no sanctions and no power*. Nor did the scheme lead to the representation of shop-floor interests at Board level or a feeling of involvement in the organization on the part of the work-force.

The study went on to suggest that the employee directors were 'subsumed into the management of BSC', losing touch with the work-force, but not gaining correspondingly any significant executive power. In making appointments, management had largely succeeded in getting people who were 'most amenable to becoming "normal", Board members' so that a shop-floor view was not heard for long in the board room.

Volvo Changes in work organization in the Swedish car industry have to be seen against a background of a near full employment economy with skilled labour in high demand. In the boom years between 1973 and 1976 the number in employment in Sweden actually rose by nearly 6 per cent. Management concern at high labour turnover, absenteeism, and the shop-floor's ability to exploit labour scarcity led to management initiatives to 'humanize' car assembly work. (This term means making work more 'human'; in other words encouraging greater job satisfaction by allowing workers to exercise initiative and responsibility.)

At the Volvo car assembly plant at Kalmar long assembly lines, like at Ford and Leyland, have been replaced by small self-contained ('autonomous') working groups who assemble entire components or sub-assemblies together. Typically, a working group will be given an assignment which is divided normally into six job sections. Each job section is carried out at a separate work station (see Figure 5). A carrier or buffer moves from one work station to another. At each station there will be two or three workers, with work cycles lasting approximately five minutes. Normally members of the working group can do the work at all six work stations and following the carrier through the whole line. In this way each worker carries out all the functions allocated to the group and performs a work cycle of twenty to thirty minutes. At Volvo, Kalmar, three-quarters of the production teams are organized for line assembly this way.

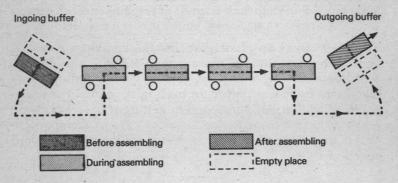

Ingoing buffer   Outgoing buffer

▨ Before assembling   ▨ After assembling

▨ During assembling   ⌐ ¬ Empty place

Figure 5   Line assembly at the Volvo factory at Kalmar

The following extract is from the 1975 Swedish Employers' Federation review of the innovations. Note especially the concentration on advanced technology and how this has been used to encourage workers to supervise their own work output in terms of both production and quality control:

Volvo invested heavily in developing the system, the key feature of which is a battery-powered wagon on which the assembly takes place. It can run a full day on its batteries, which are then recharged at night.

The painted auto bodies, made at the Volvo body factory at Gothenburg, are mounted on these wagons. The wagons then follow a system of electric 'tracks' buried in the floor, travelling almost soundlessly from one work area to another. If someone gets in the way of the wagon, it stops immediately and starts again only when the path is clear. When it comes to a work area, it stops automatically. . . The wagons are constructed so that the bodies can be turned on their side, and workers can then maintain a comfortable working position while doing assembly on the underside.

Within each work area, each of which is manned by about fifteen to twenty-five workers, there is room for six wagons. Each group can organize its work as it wishes. An individual's task time cycle can stretch up to twenty minutes, but it is also possible, if there are inexperienced workers in the group or if the group so decided, to divide the work into shorter cycles.

Each group is responsible for one homogeneous collection of assembly tasks, such as the entire electrical system. This division of the work creates completely new opportunities for concentrating on quality and decentralizing responsibility for quality. A highly developed information system continuously provides information to the members of each group on how 'their' part of each car made out at the quality checkpoints.

But what has it meant for workers? While each small group of workers is responsible for their own production targets, the pace of the line is still set by management, and the workers still complete their tasks in a set time allotted by management. Moreover, workers have found themselves doing someone else's job as well as their own. While some improvements may have been won by workers, it has been management's interests which have been best served.

We have already said that these kinds of experiments coincided with an acute labour shortage in the Swedish car industry when wage costs were very high and the demand for cars increasing. These innovations have greatly increased productivity and management has also benefited from lower labour turnover. As a recent study suggested, 'job enrichment, under the cover of humanization of the work process, was a heaven-sent strategy for squeezing more work out of the current labour-force without adding to the existing cost pressures'.

The questions raised in these two examples and particularly management's attempts to 'incorporate' trade unionism both nationally and locally are taken up and discussed further in another book in this series, *Unions and Change Since 1945* by Chris Baker and Peter Caldwell.

In this chapter we've suggested that management seeks as much control as possible over work and workers. We've taken three issues to demonstrate this – status, discipline and mechanization – all key issues in the balance of control at work. That balance has always been tilted in management's favour, and as we saw at the beginning of this chapter, management believes the time is now right to push home its advantage. Remember the interview with Len Collinson? 'The opportunity will last for two or three years. . . Then the unions will get themselves together again.' The remaining chapters of this book are concerned to show how workers and their trade unions can fight back.

Further reading

The workplace struggle for control between management and workers is perhaps best recorded in Carter L. Goddrich, *The Frontier of Control*, (Pluto Press). Although it was written in 1920, it's as relevant today as it was then.
A good recent general study is Andrew L. Friedman, *Industry and Labour* (Macmillan). Sometimes, though, its line of argument is not always easy to follow.

Other useful books are:
Hugh Beynon, *Working for Ford*, (EP Publishing)
Theo Nichols (ed), *Capital and Labour*, (Fontana)
Theo Nichols and Hugh Beynon, *Living with Capitalism*, (RKP)
Mike Cooley, *Architect or Bee? The human/technology relationship*, (Hand and Brain)

Chapter **Four**

Who's in charge?

How decisions get made

The last two chapters have looked in detail at the organization you work for. They have looked at it from two points of view:

● Who owns and controls it (your employer).
● Who runs it, and how (your management).

This chapter introduces the third factor – you, the worker. The aim is to discover who actually takes the decisions, by looking at the relationship between you and the organization which employs you: what many people call 'industrial relations'.

As Chapter one showed, that relationship consists of a power struggle – obvious at times, less obvious at others. And again as Chapter one showed, power at work is the power to get decisions implemented. In practical terms this means that the more decisions the boss can take without involving you, the more he can get away with – and the less you'll be able to do about it.

Take the case of safety at the workplace; assume the boss is considering getting you to start working with a new chemical cleaner. You've read somewhere that it can be dangerous and so you don't want to use it. What happens?

Basically, there are only three possibilities:

● The boss decides to go ahead with the chemical and you end up having to use it.
● You or your union take up the issue with the employer and negotiate a solution.
● You and your mates decide the chemical is unsafe and it doesn't get used.

In the first example management controls the situation because the decision is theirs. In the last example, it's the other way round, with you in control of what happens. The middle option is a tug of war between the two sides. The outcome depends on who has the biggest pull.

This is the test you should be applying to the decisions that matter at your workplace. Are decisions arrived at through:

● Management control?
● Bargaining for control?
● Workers' control?

The more management control decision-making the more power your boss has and the less you have. To support our claim that all decisions at work fall into one of these three categories, and to provide a way of judging what happens where you work, let's look in more detail at how decisions are reached.

Management control

The first example we gave had management taking a decision and getting it implemented. Reality may end up being like that – but it may not *look* like that. In practice, management can choose a number of ways of getting to the same point. The way they choose gives 'industrial relations' at your workplace its own particular feel. In the examples below we look at three approaches to management decision-making. Each is based on the kind of situation you could easily find yourself dealing with.

The 'bolt of lightning' approach After veiled threats about 'wage costs' from management during the annual pay talks you hear rumours about possible redundancies in your section. Your supervisor informs you in mid-week that four contract staff will start work in your section the following Monday. You are informed at the same time about the new working arrangements this will involve.

What we're describing here is one end of the spectrum – the situation where no power is shared and where decision-making is entirely a one-way process – with you at the receiving end. In Chapter three we discussed management's belief in their 'right to manage' – managerial prerogative to put it another way. Some managers take the view that once in for a penny you might as well be in for a pound. If they are there to manage and you are there to work, what's the point in beating about the bush when it's decision time? And so when the Board decides to bring in contract labour – or change stopping and starting times, or close the canteen earlier, or whatever it may be – the 'bolt of lightning' school acts first and asks questions after.

This approach is also described in the press as the 'smack of firm management' – not to be confused with union general secretaries who summarily expel members who blackleg during strikes, which the press will tend to describe as an 'outrageous attack on personal liberty'.

The 'art of communication' approach   With the annual pay settlement due, management publish a glossy, full-colour brochure showing how last year's income from trading was distributed. The brochure is mailed to workers' home addresses. It includes a picture of a large cake divided into portions for wage costs/national insurance/corporation tax/ retained for investment/dividends/operating profit. The profit 'slice' is so small as to be almost invisible. The brochure's slogan is 'Times are hard – but we'll make it if we all pull together'.

After the union submits a pay claim for 10 per cent – to match the inflation rate – every employee gets a personal letter from the Chairman. This states, at some length, that the year's financial results make a rise this size out of the question. A rise of over 6 per cent, the letter claims, will sadly mean job losses. The union are subsequently refused sight of the financial results.

By chance, the same day the local paper headlines this personal appeal by the Chairman and carries a sympathetic interview with him where he makes his case at length. A couple of days later notices are put up in every section announcing there will be a secret ballot of employees on the management offer. The next day ballot forms arrive at workers' home addresses. Accompanied by a second copy of the glossy 'Employees' Report' the ballot form says:

The company's trading position makes it unable to offer wage increases of more than 6 per cent at this time. The alternative, sadly, must be substantial loss of jobs. In view of this, are you in favour of management's offer of a 6 per cent increase on the basic rate.

YES ☐   NO ☐

Some management experts get surprisingly excited about the art of 'communication'. A number of guides have been written for managers about how to build their own 'communication systems'. Unfortunately the aim is a lot more limited than the experts realize, or admit. It is more often than not geared to getting management decisions accepted more quickly. That is certainly the intention in the kind of situation described here. Put crudely, the techniques management use in this way are weapons – in just the same way as a work to rule, go-slow, overtime ban or occupation is a weapon you can use to strengthen your position.

To be fair to management 'communicators', the example above is an extreme one. In many cases the kind of techniques used could be à step forward from the work-force's point of view. In less sensitive circumstances (than the pay rise), better communication could be very welcome. You may experience a combination of the kind of techniques the above example describes at your own workplace – such as:

- special one-off brochures;
- noticeboards;
- a 'house' journal or newspaper;
- direct mailing to your home address;
- a works loudspeaker system.

The question to ask yourself is this: how often have management communicated important information to you which is *complete* enough and *early* enough for you and the union to come up with alternatives or effective opposition? If the answer is 'frequently', you're lucky. Most shop-stewards would say they only get information about things that matter at work *once a decision has already been made* – by management. Compared to the 'bolt of lightning' approach it may be a step forward – but it's a joke for anyone to claim this means you're participating in decision-making.

The 'let's get round the table' approach Management announce they are worried about absenteeism after improvements in the sick scheme have been negotiated. They warn that as the scheme is run purely 'at the discretion of management' they are considering changing it unilaterally. As an option they offer to set up a Sick Pay Joint Consultative Committee with four stewards and two department managers. This will review absence rates and individuals' take-up of sick leave entitlement.

During JCC meetings there is a useful and frank exchange of views. Stewards point out that absenteeism is below the industry average and that the scheme's three 'waiting days' before payment is longer than in many other schemes. The two management members admit privately they think the attack on sick pay is just part of a divisional cost-cutting exercise. The JCC's final report to the plant manager notes a rise in absenteeism from 5.2 per cent to 5.7 per cent – but points to several counterbalancing factors including the newness of the scheme, a flu epidemic, and improved productivity. In a note to the report, the union representatives say the JCC findings suggest the scheme needs improving, not tightening. A month later, Divisional management announce changes in the scheme to include an extra 'waiting day', plus a new sliding scale that links the amount of sick pay you get to the absenteeism rate.

If management want to go a step further than the 'communication' approach – to get their decisions accepted – they might think in terms of the kind of approach described above. The national employers' organization, the CBI, describes this as a process of consultation: 'the means by which management seeks the views of employees before taking decisions' ('Guidelines for Action on Employee Involvement', CBI).

At your own workplace you may have come across consultation in a number of forms. Management consultants are continually coming up with different terms to describe what is essentially the same thing, for example:

Works Council
Factory Council
Company Council
Employee Council
Joint Consultative Committee
Joint Works Committee
Works Advisory Conference

The Department of Employment's research suggests that something like three out of every four workplaces will have some sort of joint consultative committee. The numbers involved in such exercises are not really important because there's no question of voting. From management's point of view, the aim is to give workers' representatives a forum where they can express their views of management plans.

Power doesn't change hands, however. As far as views and opinions are concerned consultation is two-way. But the right to take decisions stays firmly with management. To that extent unions will always look on consultation as a limited way of furthering the members' interests. For the same reason unions will generally aim to take consultation a stage further – to *negotiation*. This is what the TUC has to say about consultation:

. . . a merger between the negotiating and consultative machinery is welcome, in that it facilitates the gradual transition of matters of substance from unilateral managerial control, through consultative procedures, and eventually to become matters for negotiation. There will nevertheless be many instances where separate but compatible consultative machinery will continue to be needed, and indeed areas where new consultative machinery should be established for example in international companies.

In general there will not be a major role for separate consultative machinery but there can be important exceptions to this general conclusion.

Industrial Democracy, TUC, paragraph 67.

The TUC's message is this: however democratic consultation may *look*, it doesn't involve management handing over a scrap of their authority – any more than in the two other approaches we described earlier. That doesn't mean management won't often reach good and perfectly acceptable decisions in one or other of these ways. Because they are decisions which in effect are imposed on you, the trade union view is that *negotiation* or *bargaining* will always be a better way.

Bargaining for control

There is one key difference between consultation and bargaining. When you bargain about something there is understanding that decisions are only taken on the basis of

95

agreement. That's not to say that agreement is never reached at consultation. But if it is, it's a by-product – and a welcome one. Management enter consultation hoping your representatives will agree to their plans, but knowing they will be taking the decisions in the end whether there is agreement or not.

But in the case of negotiation, management has to *bargain* about what it wants to do. That means a decision can't be taken until one side accepts the other's point of view, or, more often, until some sort of compromise is hammered out.

The kind of compromise that emerges will very much depend on the relative strength of the two sides.

Again it is not a question of numbers. If the members are united behind a claim and backed by the union it won't matter much how few of your representatives negotiate with management. Similarly, if the members are poorly organized and divided then negotiation won't be much more of an obstacle to management than consultation. So the key distinguishing feature of negotiation is that decisions, as well as opinions, become a two-way process. Making more decisions a two-way process has always been a leading aim of trade unionism in Britain.

There are a number of forms bargaining can take, a number of ways it can affect your pay and benefits, your conditions of work, the security of your job. We look at some of these below.

I'll get the steward on to this The way the newspapers report the subject, you'd think industrial negotiations only took place between the chairmen of enterprises and union general secretaries. As far as they are concerned, Ray Buckton spends his life squeezing more pay out of British Rail, while the average shop-steward is only active when it comes to organizing strikes. As far as most stewards are concerned, predictably the media get it wrong.

Many shop-stewards – particularly those representing manual workers – have to spend much of their work – and leisure – time taking up shop-floor problems with management. Research shows that in organized workplaces, most workers with grievances take them up first with the union – i.e. their shop-steward, FOC, office representative. In *Shop-Stewards in Action*, for example, the authors found that grievances on topics like:

● overtime level;
● working conditions;
● unfair treatment;
● change in work;
● pay level;
● promotion opportunities;

'. . . would almost all be taken to the steward, or would be checked with him' by shop-floor workers. Fewer staff members take their grievances first to stewards; though roughly a fifth would do so in the case of overtime or pay level; more than half for both working conditions and unfair treatment; just under a third for a change in work; but less than one in ten for promotion opportunities. And this is only grievances!

The General and Municipal Workers' Union gives this advice to its shop-stewards on the range of topics workplace bargaining is likely to cover:

In broad terms the following range of issues should be dealt with at plant or workplace level:

● Application and interpretation in the workplace of agreements concluded at national, regional or company level.
● Breaches of agreements or established working practices.
● Piece-work and bonus rates, merit pay and individual job grading.
● Negotiation of new or modified workplace agreements on pay, conditions, procedures and so on, in consultation with your Regional Official as necessary.
● Implementation of equal pay agreements.
● Overtime working, shiftworking and manning levels.
● Holiday arrangements, canteen and general workplace welfare.
● Disciplinary and personnel matters affecting individual members.
● Emergency arrangements in the event of power failure, etc.

Shop-Stewards' Handbook, GMWU, 1975

A major survey of workplace industrial relations published in 1975 showed the variety of things stewards are expected to bargain about. We give some of the results in Table 2 below. Compare what the 'average' steward negotiates with the set-up where you work: how many of these subjects do you or your steward negotiate on individually or collectively with management? Are there other areas you or your steward bargain about, or ought to be bargaining about?

Table 2 What shop stewards bargain about

Bargaining issues	percentage of stewards surveyed who often settled these issues with management or foremen	percentage of stewards surveyed who said these issues were settled by collective agreement
Wage issues		
Basic time rates	14	56
Piece-work prices	13	22
Other forms of bonus payments	17	25
Plus payments for dirty work, etc.	6	18
Job evaluation	11	22
Merit money	5	16
Promotion or up-grading	8	20
Pensions	1	25
Working conditions		
Allocation of work	21	12
Pace of work	11	11
Quality of work	16	12
Health questions	16	21
Manning of machines	10	14
Transfer from one job to another	18	14
General conditions in workplace	37	20
Introduction of new machinery, jobs	9	13

Table 2   continued

Bargaining issues	*percentage of stewards surveyed who often settled these issues with management or foremen*	*percentage of stewards surveyed who said these issues were settled by collective agreement*
Hours of work		
Overtime arrangements	26	31
Breaks in working hours	10	29
Stopping and starting times	8	27
Holidays	14	49
Discipline		
Suspensions	1	21
Dismissals	6	22
Other disciplinary action	9	18
Employment issues		
Taking on new labour	9	12
Number of apprentices	4	12
Short time	3	13
Redundancy questions	5	27

Workplace Industrial Relations, Office of Population Censuses and Surveys, 1975

What we have described above could be called local bargaining. This can mean a shop-steward taking up some problem with supervision/management on a one-to-one basis. It can also mean sitting alongside other stewards in formal negotiations with management on (possibly) more major issues – in other words, *collective bargaining.* Collective bargaining has a national dimension too, which we deal with next.

It's all in the national agreement We're using the term 'national' agreement here to cover several types of negotiation wider than the local ones described above. These types include:

● An agreement that covers a whole *industry*. Examples are the agreements in:

Public	*Private*
British Rail	Furniture manufacturing
Post Office	Pottery industry
Coalmining	Plumbing
British Shipbuilders	Electrical contracting

● An agreement that covers an entire company, or a major section of a company such as a Product Division: there are *company-wide* agreements for:
Barclays Bank
British Home Stores
Ford Motor Company
ICI
Imperial Tobacco
Woolworths

● Agreements covering the *public service* – such as those in the:
Civil Service
Local Authorities
National Health Service
Teaching

If you're covered by a national agreement like one of these, then you know that your union, maybe together with others, negotiates at least once a year with the body representing the employer(s) about one or more aspects of your pay and conditions. You can get more of a 'profile' of your own national agreement by seeing how it compares to the three variations we discuss below.

What does the agreement cover? The starting point of most national agreements is pay – but other subjects are often included as well. Your pension, holidays, guaranteed pay, hours, premium rates, grievance procedure and job security are all things likely to be settled nationally – if you have a national agreement. It is not so likely that things like fringe benefits, plus payments, stopping and starting times, and job-related matters like speed and quality of work and manning will be covered. This is what the 'Contents' page of the water industry manual workers' agreement looks like:

CONTENTS

WAGES AND CONDITIONS OF SERVICE

Sections

101

July 1977

Not every national agreement is all-embracing like this. In some cases there is one agreement per subject – say, one covering wages and hours, another on pensions, another on job security and redundancy arrangements – all reached between the same union and employer sides. One argument for this is that it gives both sides more flexibility in what they negotiate about, and stops the entire agreement coming 'up for grabs' every time negotiations open.

Who takes part? By no means all national negotiations are conducted between national negotiators. Many are of course: when the Council of Civil Service Unions negotiates with the Government on the annual wage settlement only national officials of the unions participate. But in contrast, Ford negotiates manual workers' pay with a trade union joint body that includes company shop-stewards from its plants around Britain. Do you think it matters which arrangement applies? If so, which approach do you prefer?

Can the agreement be improved locally? National agreements don't necessarily apply rigidly all the way down the line. The Engineering Industry National Agreement is the classic example. Nationally, negotiations on manual workers' pay (and other matters) are between the Confederation of Shipbuilding and Engineering Unions and the Engineering Employers' Federation. They cover over a million workers. The eventual agreement sets a new minimum basic wage rate which should not be undercut by firms covered by the agreement. The agreement in fact sets a pay *floor*, but not a *ceiling*. What happens in practice is that local collective bargaining, as described above, frequently improves the minimum. This applies equally to the wage rate, hours, holidays and other topics in the agreement. As an example, the 1979 dispute in the industry was resolved when the employers conceded a thirty-nine-hour week from November 1981. But research at the time showed that upwards of a quarter of a million workers won local agreements to bring in a thirty-nine-hour week much sooner.

A contrasting example to the set-up in engineering is the national agreement covering NHS ancillary workers (porters, cooks, etc.). This is not generally improved on at hospital level. There are pros and cons of both arrangements and some bigger unions like the TGWU participate in both. Whatever your judgement about the benefits of these two options, at least you know the outcome is determined by straight negotiation and a trial of strength between the two sides involved. But what would happen if there was a referee? The next section provides a further variation on the bargaining theme.

Aren't we covered by a Wages Council? In one form or another Wages Councils have a long history. Their role has always been to *fix a minimum rate* (and some other conditions) in low paid and poorly organized industries where there is little or no collective bargaining. If you are in a Wages Council industry, there is a minimum wage rate your boss *must* pay you. There are Wages Councils covering these industries and services:

Aerated waters
Boot and shoe repairing
Button manufacturing
Coffin furniture and
  cerement making
Corset making
Cotton waste
Dressmaking and women's
  light clothing
Flax and hemp
Fur
General waste materials
Hairdressing
Lace finishing
Laundries
Licensed non-residential
  establishments (bars,
  pubs, etc.)
Licensed residential
  establishments (hotels,
  etc.)
Licensed restaurants

Linen, cotton handkerchief
  and household goods
Made-up textiles
Ostrich, fancy feather and
  artificial flowermaking
Prams and invalid chairs
Ready-made and wholesale
  bespoke tailoring
Retail food trades
Other (non-food) retail
  trades
Rope, twine and net-making
Rubber-proofed garment-
  making
Sacks and bags
Shirt making
Toy manufacturing
Unlicensed places of
  refreshment (canteens,
  etc.)
Wholesale mantle and
  costumes

Three groups are represented on each Wages Council: employers and unions with an interest in these industries, plus a third group of independents. These panels decide on pay

104

rates once a year and bosses throughout the industry concerned are informed of the minimum rate they should now be paying. It is bargaining of a sort in the sense that unions and employer representatives will negotiate over the size of increases. But that process is diluted because the independents must be persuaded by one side or the other to back their position. What this amounts to is employers and unions presenting a case which is then 'reviewed' by the independent members. The end result has done little to get rid of the low pay that is a feature of the Wages Council industries.

But the Councils do at least provide a wages safety-net for something like three million workers. So if you think you work in one of the industries listed, it's worth checking to make sure your boss *is* paying at least the legal minimum.

A booklet called 'Statutory minimum wages and holidays with pay' is available free from your local office of the Department of Employment and explains in more detail what Wages Councils are. To check what your present minimum pay rate should be, write to the Wages Councils Office, 12 St James Square, London, SW1; or ring 01 214 8563.

One obvious thing about the Wages Councils is that they keep your power to influence pay decisions to the minimum. A practical step you can take if your pay is fixed by one of the Councils is to think in terms of getting management to agree to an improvement on the legal minimum. The Wages Councils only establish a minimum – there is nothing to stop employers paying more.

Workers' control

So far we've worked our way across the spectrum of control at work. In the first section on *management control* we saw the different ways in which management controls the decisions that matter. In the second section on *bargaining* we showed that, in a variety of ways, negotiation breaks into management's ring of confidence and makes decisions a two-way process. At the opposite end of the spectrum are decisions taken entirely by the workers' or their representatives – in other words *workers' control*. We showed in Chapter one that:

- The British economy is still dominated by private enterprise – capitalist – employers.
- That these organizations need to operate in pyramid-fashion – from the top downwards.
- That this undemocratic way of operating has survived the growth of public sector employers like the health service, nationalized industries and so on.

Because of all this, there is correspondingly very little room for organizations that are run on different lines. This applies whether we're talking about the major decisions – such as planning, investment, marketing – or even the small ones about how sites and sections are run. But there are exceptions all the same and we look at some below.

Controlling the mini-decisions A short-term aim that has now been won in many workplaces is full union control of some of the less major decisions. In some cases management are prepared to hand over control to save themselves administrative trouble. An example is where a works committee is responsible for the works canteen, social club and other recreation facilities.

Worker-controlled *sick pay schemes* may exist because the employer refuses to set one up, or insists on unacceptable rules and conditions. There is a workers' sick pay scheme at Ford UK, for example.

We referred on page 64 to *quality circles*. These and techniques like them can give workers, probably including supervisors, some effective control over quality.

More significant issues like *recruitment, manning* and *overtime* can also be brought within union control.

Parts of the printing industry provide examples of employers using the union to fill vacancies as they come up from among the union membership. The 'gang' system on the docks has taken some decisions on manning levels out of management's hands by allowing scope for discretion between gangs of dockers, and inside gangs, on work allocation. Industries with high regular overtime provide union negotiators with a chance to regulate this too: in the health service, for example, ancillary staff stewards frequently control the amount of overtime as well as who works it.

We have put these issues under the heading of 'mini-decisions' because by no stretch of the imagination do they disturb management's overall control of jobs and work. They show that inroads can be made, however, and it is certainly a trade union aim to bring more areas under the control of workplace representatives.

Occupations Although it's essentially a defensive tactic, employees' occupation of the workplace is a classic example of workers' control. We showed in Chapter one how often workers are on the receiving end, often with no warning, of decisions they can't accept. Consultation and collective bargaining are two possible responses in that situation – occupation is a third. Broadly there are two types of occupation:

- a work-in, where the plant, office etc. is occupied and workers carry on doing their normal jobs;
- a sit-in, where there is an occupation but all work stops.

The Institute of Personnel Management (of all people!) has come up with a tighter definition:

Four main types of action of this kind can be distinguished:

Work-ins
There have been relatively few real work-ins besides the UCS example, although similar tactics have been used at Sexton's Leather Workshop in Fakenham, Norfolk, and at Briant Colour Printing. The aim is normally to demonstrate to management/government that the organization is still a viable concern where there is a proposed closure of all or part of a company.

Sit-ins over major managerial decisions
These usually take place over issues such as a closure of relatively isolated and peripheral plants by large companies and have in some cases been partially or wholly successful from the unions' point of view.

Collective bargaining sit-ins
The main example of such action is the spate of sit-ins in the Manchester area as part of the 1972 engineering industry dispute.

Tactical sit-ins
These are used as part of a wider strategy rather than as the main strategy in themselves. They can range from a half-hour sit-down at a production line to a sit-in of a few days, without taking over the factory completely. Quite often instances of this type of industrial action by workers at shop-floor level go unreported.
Sit-ins and Work-ins, IPM

A number of occupations have now proved – to anyone who doubted it – that workers are perfectly capable of running the organizations which employ them. There is not enough space in this book to do justice to the efforts of occupations that have sought to preserve jobs and services. Two examples from the Health Service (see pages 109 and 110) give an idea of what it takes to trigger an occupation, how a work-in can be sustained, and the lengths employers will go to end them.

The continuous threat to jobs means occupations are likely to spread to sectors of the economy that have little experience of them up to now. The TUC has recognized their importance as a means of combating management control of key decisions.

The relevance to industrial democracy of sit-ins and similar actions lies in the way in which imminent closures and similar events can be challenged at local level. They are local level defensive reactions to decisions on investment, closure and mergers taken elsewhere. Remote managements, attempting to take closure decisions that would blight the lives of workers (and often the prospects of whole areas and towns), can now be faced with the powerful bargaining counter of the seizure of all their assets concerned. The challenge to their unlimited property rights to do this that an occupation represents is an important consideration. The work-in variant has also been a powerful weapon, especially in the UCS situation, but this expression of workers control relates to a very special industrial and political situation, other attempts have not been so successful. Sit-ins have therefore often been a last desperate act of a work-force that has apparently reached the end of the line, and is unable to influence a decision taken elsewhere. At present, however, they are all technically illegal. The need for this form of defensive industrial action indicates the kinds of decisions that remain outside the collective bargaining process, and this pinpoints the limitation of collective bargaining.
'Industrial Democracy', TUC

Hounslow Hospital

The Hounslow Hospital is a sixty-six-bed unit with two wards, a casualty department, physiotherapy and x-ray services. The hospital was due to close on 31 July 1977, as part of a massive cutback in the area, involving six hospitals, 130 beds and over 200 jobs. Yet in one district General Hospital alone, there are 1500 surgical patients awaiting operations.

The first initiative in the campaign against the closure of Hounslow came from the Joint Shop-Stewards' Committee, covering all the hospitals in the district. On learning of the intended closure, they visited Hounslow, helped call a mass meeting, and set up a Defence Committee. The policy adopted was to follow the example of the EGA and declare a work-in to prevent closure and loss of services. The workers refused to close wards or beds, refused to accept staff transfers, and continued to accept patients. The refusal to accept staff transfers was an essential step to maintain solidarity.

The Defence Committee, with the support of the District and Area Joint Shop-Stewards' Committees, the Community Health Council, the GPs and the Unions, wanted to make the unit into a community hospital. Local GPs would then refer patients there and would themselves be able to treat them at the hospital.

However, at approximately five p.m. on Thursday 6 October, a squad of private ambulances and vans, accompanied by police and health officers, swooped on the wards of Hounslow Hospital, seized the full complement of patients, and bundled them in to the waiting transport, which took them to the West Middlesex Hospital. The patients, mainly geriatric, were manhandled in a manner which may have gravely affected their health. This body-snatching operation, unprecedented in the history of the Health Service, took place as a desperate attempt to end the work-in at Hounslow Hospital. The work-in attracted widespread attention and become a nationally recognized focus of the fight to defend the NHS. The lifting of the patients was carried out in the face of mounting opinion for reconsideration of the original decision to close Hounslow Hospital. The local Community Health Council had declared themselves in favour if its retention as a community hospital, and a resolution was moved to this effect at the meeting of the Area Health Authority on 12 October. The unions are currently demanding an enquiry into the events of 6 October.

Basil Bye and Nick Bradley, 'Occupation', Southern Region Trade Union Information Unit.

The Weir Hospital

The Merton, Sutton and Wandsworth Area Health Authority decided to close the Weir Maternity Hospital, Weir Road, Balham. They wanted to close it so they could turn the buildings into *offices*.

The threatened closure was the direct result of the Government's cuts in public spending. To meet official targets, the Health Authority slashed its budget this year by three-and-a-half million pounds.

The management had already started to reduce the number of staff at the hospital in order to make it easier to close.

On Friday 20 May, the ancillary and nursing staff of the Weir Maternity – who are all members of NUPE – decided to occupy the hospital to prevent its proposed closure. The hospital was kept open and was being run in a responsible and very efficient manner. The doctors and consultants were performing their normal duties. The occupation showed that the workers are capable of running their own services and industries.

The Weir Maternity Hospital in South West London was under occupation for a time and was the subject of a vigorous campaign involving all the hospitals in the district. The occupation was organized by ancillary and nursing staff in NUPE.

They received active support from the union and the local branch. A tremendous amount of local support was given, but the campaign was not successful in keeping the hospital going as a maternity unit. Unfortunately nursing and medical staff began taking up posts elsewhere, leaving it to the ancillary workers to fight on.

The Merton, Sutton and Wandsworth Area Health Authority steadfastly refused to change their minds on the closure, which was part of the three-and-a-half million pound cuts in the Area. The latest position is that it may still close, without even a guarantee that it will be used as some other form of hospital. It may be converted to offices!

Basil Bye and Nick Bradley, 'Occupation', Southern Region Trade Union Information Unit.

Workers' co-operatives The third variant on workers' control in operation is workers' co-operatives. Co-operatives are attracting a growing interest – again the threat to jobs has been the spur. But what exactly are co-operatives?

This is how the Labour Party has defined them:

'The essential characteristics of the workers' co-operative are that it manufactures goods or provides services and that it is owned and controlled by those working in it.'

The Labour Party adds the rider that co-operatives should fulfil these three conditions:

- such organizations must be controlled on a one member–one vote basis;
- anyone who participates in such an organization should, after meeting the necessary qualifications, have a right to membership;
- the interest paid on any share and loan capital must not exceed the amount needed to obtain and retain that capital.

Workers' Co-operatives, Labour Party

There is nothing new about the co-operative idea. Their history goes back to co-operative corn mills in the late eighteenth century, and in the nineteenth century to Robert Owen's mill at New Lanark. By the end of the last century there were something like a hundred co-operatives. In this century, the big growth in co-operatives has occurred over the last ten years and there are now estimated to be some 300 industrial and service co-operatives in the UK. They operate in engineering, electronics, chemicals, footwear and clothing manufacture, retailing, printing, building, furniture-making and other sectors. Most are small, typically employing less than twenty people.

This is how one co-operative was set up, following the closure of a Courtaulds factory:

Around lunchtime today a delivery truck will arrive in a Grantham side street, dwarfing the Old Bakery where it stops. A couple of dozen workers, including the entire managerial staff, will bring out hundreds of dresses and skirts loaded on hangers.

111

There are no miserable faces among the workers. Grantham Workers' Co-operative has completed its fifth full week in production.

'That's the thing about co-ops,' says Ann Griffiths. 'We all have our own jobs – I'm a presser – but we lend a hand where it's needed.' For Celia Wadey – by common consent the driving force behind the idea of a co-op – her best moment in their short history came as she left one woman to work on after everybody else had left. 'Of course I'll be all right,' the woman told her. 'If anyone comes I'll fight to defend this place. After all, part of it belongs to me.'

The enthusiasm at Grantham Fashions is almost missionary. 'If anyone came to us saying they were thinking of setting up a co-op I would tell them to get on with it,' says Geoffrey Fincham, cutter, designer and one of the three men on the co-op's twenty-seven strong work-force.

'I only wish there were more help available to people who wanted to do it,' he said.

The co-op knows just how important it is to get help and just how disheartening it can be to have to overcome what seem like needless obstacles. But now, with a grant from the Job Creation Programme, the co-op's future is guaranteed for at least a year. The members were among 180 workers made redundant when the town's Courtaulds clothing factory announced its closure in autumn 1976. They spent the best part of a year on the dole, while trying to raise money to get the co-op on its feet. On top of the usual fund-raising one of the best things to happen to them was the Silver Jubilee – Celia Wadey and Geoff Fincham spent a week stitching up bunting and raised an extra £100. . .

Many of their old colleagues are still on the dole or have simply given up working altogether. But Ms Wadey, then National Union of Hosiery and Knitwear Workers shop-steward, had no intention of losing the skills accumulated at the old factory. . .

Ms Wadey started lobbying her fellow workers 'Some of them thought I was mad, but about thirty-five seemed to take to the idea.' In the following months some of the original workers dropped out, but those who remain are now firmly wedded to the idea. . .

A committee of eight who meet once a week make recommendations on managerial decisions to the monthly staff meetings. Sometimes the general meetings accept the advice and sometimes they don't. But because everyone plays a part there is no argument when decisions have been made, said Geoff Fincham.

Grantham Fashions has had plenty of help. The Institute for Workers' Control, the Industrial Common Ownership Movement and co-op expert Professor John Beishon of the Open University have all given advice and encouragement. Their union has helped them get orders and several unions have sent cash.

Perhaps less predictably, both the local manager of Barclays Bank and Council officers have provided crucial help.

The Manpower Services Commission, responsible to the Government for the Job Creation Programme, is viewed in more ambiguous light. The commission is paying the £100,000 which guarantees the co-op for a year.

Workers Control Bulletin, No 2, 1978

What is the attraction of a co-operative – other than as a possible means of saving jobs? Think back to Chapter one's discussion of management control over jobs and work. We said there that your vulnerability as a worker stems from the fact that your job is *owned* by your employer – despite the fact that it's your labour which keeps the business or service alive. What this means for industrial relations, we argued, is that conflict between management and managed will always be on or just below the surface.

Co-operatives, or workers' self-management, offers an alternative to this. Turn back to the pools win story on page 15 and to our question about the way profit is distributed in a normal business. And then consider this extract – also on profit – about co-ops.

In a workers' co-operative a clear distinction should be drawn between reward for capital and reward for labour. Those who provide capital should receive a fair reward for doing so in the form of interest at an agreed rate, but any trading surplus which remains after the payment of this interest is regarded as having been created by the efforts of the work-force. It should therefore be regarded as a reward for these efforts, to be used as the work-force decide and not for the further reward of those who provide the capital. In traditional terms, loan stock is permissible but ordinary stock is not, and this principle is often expressed as 'labour hires capital, capital does not hire labour'.

Control can hardly be said to lie with the work-force if it is possible for the enterprise to be 'sold up' without their consent, and it is therefore customary to stipulate that, whatever the form of ownership structure, the enterprise cannot be dissolved except with the consent of the members and that even then the assets realized shall not be distributed to the members. (emphasis added)

Workers Co-operatives, Aberdeen People's Press

The co-operative system also offers a clear alternative to the kind of management most workers experience, which we described in Chapter three. We gave on page 18 one alternative view of what management's role could be; the same book explains the possible ways management can be provided in a workers' co-operative.

There are three basic options. First and ideally, the people who do 'management' jobs will be elected to do them by a vote of the whole work-force or by a sub-committee of the work-force. Second, if by general agreement some control is still retained by the founding group, it may be agreed that one or more of that group, though not formal members of the co-operative, shall be responsible for one or more of these jobs, and in the early years of a co-operative where there is goodwill and common sense the work-force sometimes prefer this arrangement. Third, management can be hired; i.e. people with the appropriate skills not possessed by the members, who are not members of the co-operative and who do not wish to become so, are employed by the co-operative to manage the commercial, but *not* the co-operative aspects of its affairs.

Who decides what?

This chapter has posed the question, who takes the decisions, by showing that the whole range of decision-making can be looked at under three broad headings: management control, collective bargaining, workers' control.

In this final section we suggest that you consider issues which affect you at work, and assess who decides what. The list in Table 3 (on page 116) doesn't cover everything, but is a rough-and-ready guide to the areas where, directly or indirectly, you have a stake in what management decides. The questions are geared to help you weigh up how much control you have over those areas. As you'll see, the questions we ask about your management leave out the worker control option. This is not because we consider it an impractical pipedream – the examples above show that's not the case. But if you're weighing up the balance of power *now* at work, it's odds on that the questions we ask at the top of each column cover all the options open to you.

If you work for a typical employer you should find fewer ticks in the two right-hand columns and more in the two left-hand columns, as you work your way down the list. By the time you get down to the decisions about 'The enterprise' – the really major decisions – it's probable that you're not even being consulted by management before decisions are taken. Yet we've shown in Chapters one and two that you have a vital interest in what gets decided at that level.

How many of the decisions we've listed can you see yourself and your union getting more control over? It could be simply a question of winning consultation about management's plans where none existed before. It could be forcing management to add to the number of non-wage benefits they bargain about. It could be bringing more aspects of the job and of working conditions under your and the union's control (see page 106). It could be negotiating an information disclosure agreement on top level plans (see the model agreement on page 47).

In the next chapter we talk about the ways you'll need to build up your organization at work to make these steps a practical possibility.

Further reading

You'll find all the books we listed at the end of Chapter one relevant to the things this chapter has talked about too. But directly linked to the theme of bargaining and control are the following books, whose titles speak for themselves:

C. Jenkins and B. Sherman *Collective Bargaining* (Routledge and Kegan Paul, 1977).

Table 3

Decisions on	Subject	How are decisions reached in your workplace?			
		By management without any consultation?	By management after consultation?	After negotiations outside the workplace?	After negotiation at the workplace?
The wage packet	Basic pay	☐	☐	☐	☐
	Overtime and shift pay	☐	☐	☐	☐
	Bonus pay	☐	☐	☐	☐
Non-wage benefits	Holidays	☐	☐	☐	☐
	Sick pay and injury benefit	☐	☐	☐	☐
	Occupational pension	☐	☐	☐	☐
	Maternity	☐	☐	☐	☐
	Paternity	☐	☐	☐	☐
	Allowances/perks	☐	☐	☐	☐
	Job security	☐	☐	☐	☐
	Special leave	☐	☐	☐	☐
	Nursery/crèche provision	☐	☐	☐	☐
	Guaranteed week	☐	☐	☐	☐
	Medical and welfare	☐	☐	☐	☐
	Time off	☐	☐	☐	☐
Working conditions	Hours (breaks, stopping/starting times, etc)	☐	☐	☐	☐

☐☐☐☐☐☐   ☐☐☐☐☐☐☐☐☐   ☐☐☐☐☐☐☐☐☐

☐☐☐☐☐☐   ☐☐☐☐☐☐☐☐☐   ☐☐☐☐☐☐☐☐☐

☐☐☐☐☐☐   ☐☐☐☐☐☐☐☐☐   ☐☐☐☐☐☐☐☐☐

☐☐☐☐☐☐   ☐☐☐☐☐☐☐☐☐   ☐☐☐☐☐☐☐☐☐

Discipline
Grievances
Safety
Health
Recreation and refreshment
Facilities (lockers, toilets, phone-boxes, etc.)

The job
Payment system
Grading and re-grading
Manning
Flexibility/mobility
Speed of work
Quality of work
Type of machinery
Training
Job environment (space/heat/noise/light, etc.)

The enterprise
Manpower
Investment
Research and development
Sales and trading plans
Production plans
Profit
Dividends
Financial planning
Mergers/closures/takeovers

A. Campbell and J. McIlroy *Getting Organized* (Pan Books, 1981), in the same series as this book.

Workers' Co-operatives: A Handbook (Aberdeen People's Press, 1980).

Workers' Co-operatives (Labour Party, 1980).

K. Coates *Work-ins, Sit-ins and Industrial Democracy* (Spokesman Books, 1981).

Chapter **Five**

Building union organization

So far we've looked at how the balance of control at work favours employers. We've seen how work is organized to meet employers' requirements which are determined largely by the profit motive. In the last chapter we argued that one way forward for the trade union movement was to challenge the notion that workers should limit their collective bargaining objectives to a narrow shopping list of bread-and-butter issues. We argued forcefully for extending collective bargaining into every aspect of working life. That approach cannot succeed unless it is accompanied by improvements in trade union organization at the workplace level and beyond. This is not a criticism of present trade union structures, far from it. But improvements in trade union organization are essential if workers are to effectively defend their organizations and challenge management's control of work. As employers become more sophisticated in their approaches and organizationally stronger, so the trade union movement must do the same.

This chapter then, is about opening up new possibilities for trade union organization, broadening horizons if you like. It does this in two ways. First, we look at how workers, through different forms of trade union organization, have reacted to the problems thrown up by modern company structures and management methods. Second, we suggest how workers in practical terms can beef-up their organizations to make them more effective. But it's not just a question of preparing for the big set-piece struggles. What we have to say here is relevant to every issue at the work-place where the question of control is central.

Organizing into branches

All trade union organization is built from the base – the members – upwards. The strength of any union is its members, but the membership must be effectively organized before that strength can be effectively used.

The most basic form of trade union organization is the branch. As a trade unionist you will be a member of a branch which will be either *residential based* or *workplace based*:

● The members of the branch may all work at *the same trade* for *the same employer*.
● The members of the branch may work at *different trades* but for *the same employer*.
● The members of the branch may work in *the same trade* but for *different employers*.
● The members of the branch may work at *different trades* and for *different employers*.

The first two categories are *workplace branches*. The second two categories are *residential branches*.

There will be many good administrative, organizational and policy reasons why your branch is structured the way it is and it would be worthwhile finding out what they are. But does one type of branch have major advantages over the other?

The argument for *residential* branches is that they provide a meeting place where workers from different workplaces and jobs can meet to exchange their experiences. In other words the residential branch provides a much wider forum for the discussion of common issues and a basis for solidarity across workplaces.

The supporters of *workplace* branches argue that workers identify first and foremost with their workplace. They say that for this reason trade union organization at local level should reflect the unit of work organization most familiar to workers, the workplace. This is how a report to the 1980 Biennial General Meeting of the National Union of Seamen saw the argument:

If members do not come to the Union or branch, then we should take the Union or branch to the members on ships. We have to shift Union power to the ships and this means creating shipboard branches giving Union representatives the ability to negotiate their own agreements.

In its handbook for shop-stewards the TGWU has described the role of the branch in the following way:

The branch is the place where the rank and file member has a chance to make his contribution to the Union's policy. It is the springboard of union democracy. On the floor of the branch, local decisions are made which may then be transmitted through the dual machinery of the Union. Industrial matters go through the regional trade group machinery; administrative matters are sent to the Regional Committee. High policy resolutions, and resolutions to change the rules of the Union may also be sent to the Biennial Delegate Conference and the Rules Conference. In its turn, the branch is the point of transmission of the Union's policy to the membership. Here, members are informed of the decisions of the

121

governing bodies. It is, therefore, a vital part of the Union's machinery. Its liveliness is a measure of the vitality of the whole Union.

The branch, be it workplace or residential, is firstly an *administrative* or business unit. It will consider applications for membership and it may be the collecting point for union dues. It is certainly a financial unit in that, besides collecting dues and defraying them to district, regional or national level, it will, within defined limits, have the right to authorize expenditure from branch funds for appropriate purposes like local campaigns.

The branch is also an *information* unit. The branch is a forum which allows members to exchange views and opinions. It is also a channel for information *from* higher levels within the union and *to* higher levels within the union.

Finally, the branch has a decisive role in determining and applying union *policy*. The effective operation of trade union democracy depends upon informed discussion at branch level. Ideas first discussed at fortnightly or monthly branch meetings may, in due course, become *national* union policy. Through the system of representative government, common to all trade union organization and involving delegate conferences, policy is determined by the membership. And while there is a responsibility on union members to be active in determining policy, there is also a common duty on union members to ensure the proper implementation of policies that have been democratically determined.

Building workplace organization

On the job the branch, by its very nature, cannot defend workers' interests all the time. That role is reserved for shop-stewards who are elected by their workmates to act on their behalf in representing their interests to their employer.

Trade union workplace representatives, now generally referred to as shop-stewards, have existed in British industry for many years. The first big boost to this form of trade union workplace organization came during the First World War amongst engineering workers on Clydeside. Further impetus came from workers' opposition to government attempts at controlling and directing labour during the Second World War, but it was the 1960s and the rise of productivity bargaining that brought this form of trade union organization to most sectors of the economy. The term *shop-steward* is the most widely used, but other terms are in use in different industries, amongst which we can include:

Fathers and mothers of chapel (printing);
Corresponding members (among engineering draughtsmen);
Local Department Committee members (railways);
The term Office representative or Staff representative is often used in white collar employment.

Today there are probably not less than 300,000 shop-stewards in British industry. We've said that their primary responsibility is to represent their workmates' interests to their employer which they do as *trade union officers*, appointed by and answerable to those they represent.

In the white collar union APEX the functions and duties of the Staff representative are defined like this:

The staff representative is the first line of communication and activity for a member of the union . . . (he or she) has a number of basic duties which can be summarized as the following:

i) to ensure that existing agreements affecting APEX members are being observed;
ii) to represent members in domestic grievances to management;
iii) to submit proposals for improved conditions to the Area Official;
iv) to act as authorized by the Area Official in discussing improvements in conditions with management;
v) to advise members on employment matters;
vi) to keep the branch secretary informed of developments;
vii) to provide information about APEX to members;
viii) to call when necessary and with the approval of the branch officers, meetings of the staff he or she covers;
ix) to create and maintain interest in the Union amongst members;
x) to take action where necessary to prevent arrears in contributions and lapses of membership.

123

In very general terms then the role of the shop-steward can be broken down under the following headings:

Representing the membership and bargaining on behalf of the membership with management.

Communicating with the membership on behalf of the union and communicating with the union on behalf of the membership.

We're going to concentrate on how the steward's *representative* role has developed. We'll illustrate this by looking at the growth of shop-floor organization in the public services.

The National Union of Public Employees (NUPE) only introduced shop-stewards in the 1960s, winning recognition for them in local government in 1969, and in the National Health Service in 1971. Today there are probably 10,000 manual workers' shop-stewards in local government. One of the major problems of plant level organization in a sector like local government is the way the work-force tends to be located in widely dispersed small groups. NUPE clearly recognized the major organizational problems involved in establishing steward organization, but nonetheless remained convinced of its necessity. In its 1979 review of the development of shop-steward organization NUPE identified as a major influence the need for workers to exercise greater control over decision-making at work.

It is no coincidence that the past few years should have witnessed the development of a strong tendency towards the growth of union stewards within NUPE. . . In the first place there has been an opening up of opportunities for local bargaining. . . The increasing use of modern management techniques, particularly workstudy-based incentive schemes and productivity bargains, has introduced a new dimension into the Union's work. While the broad frames of reference for such agreements can be established at national level the critical task of fitting them into particular circumstances can only be done at the workplace, and with a high degree of involvement by workers on the job. . .

The second factor prompting the development of union stewards is the development of services in which NUPE members are employed. In size, structure and scope, the local government and health services are growth industries. . .

The practical results are well known to every NUPE member. The time lag in between raising an issue and getting an answer becomes longer. Real managers – those with the power to make decisions – become increasingly remote from the work-force. . .

In response to this situation, Union members at the workplace push management harder in an effort to break down the communications barrier. This is a spontaneous reaction which encourages the growth of confidence in local work-groups and promotes the emergence of articulate spokesmen who argue the workers' case with management: instant stewards, in fact.

Another important factor in promoting the development of stewards within NUPE is the growth of the Union itself . . . the sheer size of the Union poses the need to develop organizational forms which preserve and extend the democratic character of the Union.

So then, three developments – new opportunities for local bargaining, the growth of the public sector, and a corresponding increase in membership – combined together to encourage the development of a shop-steward system. In these circumstances the shop-steward was seen as a necessary reponse to more sophisticated management structures and techniques, and to the challenge of maintaining and extending democracy within the union.

Getting stewards together

With the exception of the very smallest workplaces with only two or three shop-stewards, some form of collective shop-steward organization has developed throughout industry. The most common type of steward organization is the Joint Shop-Stewards Committee (JSSC for short), involving all stewards employed in the same plant. Since the Second World War the JSSC has been the key unit of trade union organization throughout manufacturing industry, and is becoming increasingly important in other sectors of the economy as well. High levels of employment after the War strengthened the position of those JSSCs already in existence and encouraged the creation of many others. In 1947 the Confederation of Shipbuilding and Engineering Unions

(CSEU) gave official backing to JSSCs by providing for Confederation or Inter-Union Committees, with credentials issued by the CSEU District Committees. It's important to remember that in many workplaces more than one union exists, so a method has to be found for bringing together the representatives of workers from different unions. At least 50 per cent of manual workers' establishments and 30 per cent of non-manual establishments have more than one union. The JSSC is a way of resolving this problem.

Typically in small plants all the shop-stewards will meet regularly together as a committee. In larger plants it is usual for the senior shop-stewards or convenors representing individual unions, departments or sections of the plant to meet as an executive body of the JSSC. Such an executive body is responsible for all interdepartmental or plant level negotiations with management. The works convenor usually acts as secretary to the JSSC, and will often work full-time on union business, paid and provided with office and secretarial facilities by the firm.

What then are the advantages of this form of shop-floor organization? Firstly, the JSSC represents the collective strength of all workers within the plant. Secondly, JSSCs allow the collective *experiences* of the workplace to be drawn together. Thirdly, and this follows from the first two points, the JSSC can decide on and pursue collective *tactics* and collective *action*. As unity is strength, so unity based on shop-floor representative democracy provides the most effective means of pushing forward the interests of workers.

How can shop-steward organization be made more effective?

To make workplace organization *effective* organization shop-stewards individually and collectively require certain supporting services. The TUC has suggested that the following facilities are the minimum which can be reasonably expected of management:

● The provision of a list of new entrants to the appropriate trade union representatives.

126

- Facilities on the premises for shop-stewards to explain to each new worker the advantages of trade union membership together with the terms of the collective agreements covering the establishment.
- Facilities to collect union contributions or to inspect members' cards or the operation of a check-off system where this is desired by unions.
- Facilities either in the form of a room or at the minimum a desk in the workplace (in the case of a senior shop-steward a separate office would probably be desirable) together with adequate facilities for storing correspondence and papers. All stewards should have ready access to telephones and to typing and duplicating facilities.
- The provision of a notice-board and the use of an internal post system.
- The use of a suitable room for the purpose of consulting and reporting to members when necessary during working hours and for meetings of shop-steward committees.
- Sufficient time off with pay at average earnings during working hours for a steward to:

  perform all his/her union duties which relate to the workplace;

  attend training courses in industrial relations where syllabuses have been approved by his/her union and/or the TUC;

  attend conferences called by his/her union. The steward should not have to use holiday entitlement for this purpose.

These are not pie-in-the-sky demands, they can be won. A Labour Research Department survey of 142 employers in 1979 showed that the great majority of stewards had got the facilities recommended by the TUC. The survey also showed that by hard bargaining many stewards had obtained a wide range of other facilities beyond those recommended by the TUC. For example these are the facilities won by staff representatives at the Acton plant of Lucas CAV:

1 The use of an internal telephone. The Senior Staff Representative may also use a Company external telephone.

2 The use of an office or conference room for interviews of a private nature.

3 The use of notice-boards (yet to be provided) for posting Union information. This facility may be shared with other staff unions.

4 The provision of a filing cabinet for the Senior Staff Representative.

5 The provision of a desk for the Senior Staff Representative if the nature of his work is such that he has no desk of his own.

6 The deduction of Union dues at source together with permission to collect dues not deducted at source.

7 Permission to hold elections for staff representatives in Company time and on Company premises providing that prior arrangements have been made with the Personnel Manager.

8 Permission to hold general meetings for reporting back following national negotiations or for discussing other major issues providing that prior arrangements have been made with the Personnel Manager.

9 The reasonable use of typing, duplicating, stationery services etc.

10 The introduction of new employees to the appropriate local Staff Representatives.

11 The opportunity of talking to trainees as set out in the Procedure Agreement covering trainees these arrangements to be made through the Personnel Manager.

12 Access to copies of executive memorandas held in the Personnel Department which deal with management appointments.

13 The opportunity for the Senior Staff Representative to inspect job specifications for those jobs within his Union's sphere of influence.

14 The training of staff representatives to be carried out in Company time and with no loss of pay.

Bargaining Report No. 5, Labour Research Department, 1979

Take another look at the last item on the TUC list and the demand for paid time off. What's being said here is that for stewards to perform their duties effectively trade union training is essential. With the passing of the Employment Protection Act in 1975 shop-stewards have the legal right to reasonable paid time off during working hours to perform their industrial relations duties. They also have the right to paid time off to undertake trade union training to extend their skills and knowledge as stewards. An ACAS Code of Practice issued under the Act says that:

Training should be relevant to the industrial relations duties of an official (e.g. shop-steward). It should be approved by the TUC or the official's union. . .

An official who has duties concerned with industrial relations should be permitted to take reasonable paid time off work for initial basic training . . . (and) . . . further training . . . where he or she has special responsibilities or where such training is necessary to meet circumstances such as changes in the structure or topics of negotiation . . . or legislative changes.

By negotiating with management for the facilities suggested and by extending through collective bargaining the time-off provisions, shop-stewards can further equip themselves with the tools of their trade and gain greater understanding in their more effective use.

But it has to be remembered that unless good communication is maintained with the shop-floor, no steward can be an effective representative. Shop-stewards are responsible to the members who elect them and it is essential that they remain constantly sensitive to the wishes and feelings of their members.

How to combat the big monopolies

The big monopolies have tentacles which stretch into every corner of our lives. Their activities affect us as workers and consumers. The following sketch illustrates their wide-ranging activities and suggests that any trade union response has to come to terms with the fact that in all likelihood the big monopolies will not be single-product or single-location enterprises.

DEMOCRACY AT WORK

The story . . .

It's seven o'clock Friday morning and Maggie and Dennis get up for work. Dennis works at *Mono Pumps*, an engineering firm, while Maggie works at the local *Samuel Jones* paper mill.

After washing and drying themselves on *Fieldcrest* towels, they each have an *Eastwood* boiled egg for breakfast. Then it's off to work after arranging to meet later that afternoon to do the weekend shopping. On his way to the bus stop Dennis stops off at the local *Forbouy's* newsagent to get a paper and at the *Finlay's* tobacconist to get some *Condor* for his new *Charatan* pipe.

In the canteen at lunchtime Dennis decides on a meal of *Ross* frozen fish, chips made of *Sun King* potatoes, and *Smedley's* tinned peas, all generously laced with *HP* sauce. For afters it's *Tudor Dairy* ice cream. Maggie has contented herself with a bag of *Golden Wonder* crisps.

After work Maggie and Dennis meet in the High Street. They've got a good selection of shops in their town – there's an *International Stores* supermarket, *F. J. Wallis*, *MacMarket*, *Argos* discount store, *Star Cash and Carry*, and *Saccone & Speed* and *Arthur Cooper* off-licences.

While Maggie goes to the International Stores, Dennis goes to the local *Dolland & Aitchison* opticians to see if his new spectacles are ready. He then visits Arthur Cooper, the off-licence. On Saturday it's their wedding anniversary, so they're having a party with a few friends. Dennis orders three bottles of *Glen Grant* whisky, three bottles of *Burne Turner* gin and two dozen cans of *Colt 45*.

Maggie has already bought Dennis a gold signet ring from *Collingwoods*, the West End jewellers, when she was in London a few weeks back. She's also bought him a bottle of *Lentheric* aftershave.

Dennis has bought Maggie a bracelet from *Aspreys* together with some *Yardley* and *Morney* cosmetics. On top of that he's arranged for the florist to deliver a large bunch of flowers from *Lowland Nurseries*.

After dinner that evening – a salad of cold *Buxted* chicken and *Epicure* pickles – they pop down to their local *Courage* pub. While Dennis is waiting to be served he notices the wide range of beers on offer – Courage and *John Smith* ales, *Harp*, *Kronenburg* and *Carling* lagers. Maggie, meanwhile is getting a packet of *Silk Cut* from the *Mayfair* vending machine. Dennis decides to treat himself to a *Reetmeister* Dutch cigar. Over their drinks they discuss their *Ladbroke-Courage* holiday which they've just booked for next summer.

One more drink and they decide to go home. Before going to bed, Maggie remembers she has forgotten to write to her sister in America who works for New York's biggest fashion store, *Saks*. She puts her *Montblanc* pen to *Wiggins Teape* writing paper and thinks how sad it is that her sister has been away for so long. And so to bed. . .

Of course 'Maggie' and 'Dennis' are fictitious characters, but the story is more 'faction' than fiction. Every commodity brand, every retail outlet, and all the companies mentioned have the following in common. They're all part of the vast empires of Britain's four leading tobacco companies – Gallahers, Rothmans, Imperial and British American Tobacco. As they say, 'from tiny acorns. . .'

Rightly as *consumers* we are concerned at the growth in power and influence of the big monopoly companies. Also, the monopolies pose both a threat and a challenge to *trade unionists*. How then can the trade union movement fight back?

Building the combine

So far we have concentrated on shop-steward organization within single plants. But many workers are employed in multi-plant and multi-product enterprises. For example, Figure 6 shows the locations, manpower distribution, divisions and main products of ICI, Britain's largest industrial company. Are there ways then by which workplace organization can be extended beyond the individual plant to cover all plants within the common ownership of a multiplant company, a big monopoly or a state enterprise? One group of trade unionists has posed the problem this way:

'How can our shop-floor power be strengthened and our trade union structures be reformed so that we do have the power to challenge central management's decisions on investment, technology, products, pensions and other major company-wide issues?'

Because individual JSSCs have found it impossible to combat management strategies sometimes arrived at on a national basis, it has been necessary to organize across workplaces. The 1950s and 1960s saw the development of Joint Shop-Stewards Combine Committees on both an *industry-wide* (e.g. docks) and a *company-wide* (e.g. Leyland) basis.

Such Combine Committees have often resulted from particular crises within the industry or company. Often their beginning has been an exchange of correspondence between

Figure 6 ICI locations and manpower distribution

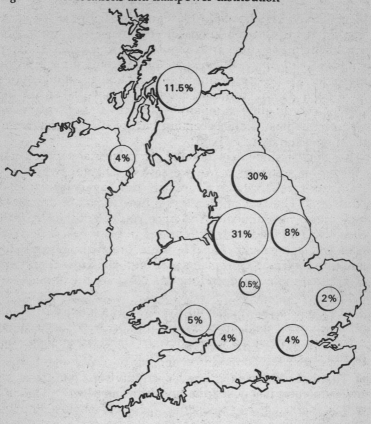

ICI's divisions and main products

Agricultural	Fertilizers, industrial chemicals, catalysts
Fibres	Nylon and polyester fibres
Mond	Plastics monomers, chlorinated solvents, alkalis, acids, salt, chlorine, lime, titanium
Organics	Dyes, pigments, rubber chemicals, urethanes, detergents, silicones
Paints	Decorative and industrial paints, wallpapers
Petrochemicals	Olefines, aromatics, glycols, phenol, dimethylterephthalate, nylon 6:6 salt
Pharmaceuticals	Medical and veterinary drugs
Plant Protection	Herbicides, fungicides, pesticides, seed dressing
Plastics	Plastic resins and products

Total number employed in the UK in 1979 was 89,400
Derived from Joe Pecker, *Social changes at Work*

plant JSSCs. This has led to a regular exchange of information on terms and conditions of employment. More formal organization has come with regular meetings, officers, constitutions and financial levies on the constituent parts of the combine. Where company-wide bargaining arrangements have been absent, combine committees have taken on the role of coordinating company-wide activities. In some instances this has meant becoming part of the national negotiating machinery (e.g. Ford).

But don't assume that combine committees are appropriate only to big enterprises. As we saw in Chapter two, many companies, relatively small in size, can have very complex structures. The task of identifying how firms are organized may prove very difficult. And once you've got the structure clear you may find wide differences in plant customs, practices and agreements. Despite these problems the case for building the combine remains a strong one. How then have combine committees been formed? What are the obstacles to overcome?

In 1976 a working party of the Tyne Conference of Shop-Stewards published a practical guide on how to go about setting up a combine committee. In their report they suggested that there were four initial stages:

● The first task was to correctly identify your employer.
● The second task was to locate all the employer's plants.
● The third stage was to establish what the employer's plans and policies were.
● The fourth stage was to make contact with other workers employed by your employer.

In Chapter two we considered many of the questions which arise from these first three stages (see pages 28–56). The fourth stage, making contact with other workers, poses the most difficult problems of all. This is what the Tyne group had to say on this:

Many obstacles can rear their heads here – including management harassment (refusal to let phones be used, pass on letters addressed to the 'Senior Shop-Stewards', etc.), suspicion on the part of official district organizers (if you try going through the formal channels), etc. You should, of course, try these channels, but a bit more detective work may well be needed. Here, things such as trade union directories may be of assistance. If your union has such a thing (the AUEW has), it may well list the names and addresses of branch secretaries throughout the land. If so, you may be able to identify the name of a branch secretary living in the near vicinity of a particular plant you wish to contact. If so, try writing/phoning to say you'd like to contact the convenor or shop-stewards' representative at such and such a plant . . . etc. (this has paid off on occasions in our experience). The name and address of a contact in the plant is far better than a letter addressed to the Shop-Stewards Committee at the plant, as it may well not arrive. . .

If the initial soundings prove favourable to the idea (obviously nothing like 100 per cent response will occur at first), and convenors'/shop-stewards' committees have the support of the workers in going ahead, a meeting in a centrally accessible place will be needed, to discuss further the issues of concern common to all, the general exchange of information, and the means of constructing a Combine Committee capable of taking up some of the issues. Here, constitutions, membership fees, travel allowance (which often need to be pooled as stewards will travel varying distances and incur greater or lesser expenses) will need to be sorted out. Relationships with the official side of the movement, too, will need to be sorted out. And of course, strategies and policies.

To date there are probably some thirty combine committees in Britain operating largely, but not exclusively in the engineering industries. Some like the Lucas Aerospace stewards have gained a justified reputation for developing radically new approaches to the traditional problems facing workers. In January 1980, representatives from fourteen different combines met to discuss the common problems of redundancies, new technology, and the growing management offensive against shop-floor organization. Here was clear evidence that the argument for combine committees was being taken a stage further. Discussion focused on building a national network of combines as a means of developing co-operation *between* combines. During the year a *Joint Forum of Combine Committees* was formed and in October, under the signature of seven combines (British Aerospace, Dunlop, Lucas Aerospace, Metal Box, Power Engineering, Thorn/EMI, and Vickers) put forward these following guiding principles for extending combine power:

Multi-union involvement
In order to build a strong organization and create unifying policies it is vital to seek the active involvement of all sections of the work-force, staff as well as manual, women as well as men and so on. Only in this way can a combine committee fight to exert control over every aspect of management's activity. The coming together of these different sections can lead to an invaluable learning process. Through this, sectional disagreements and misunderstandings can be overcome, however slow and painful the process may be.

Rank and file involvement
The most important problem facing a combine committee, like any other trade union organization, is that of convincing the membership of the need to act collectively. This means the combine committee has to gain practical credibility in the eyes of the membership.

For this, it is important for the combine-wide contact to produce small gains, if only through exchanging information. And the combine needs a newspaper or bulletin to report these successes back to the membership. It also needs to establish a procedure for discussion of items on the combine committee's agenda among the shop-stewards and their sections before the meeting as well as after.

This procedure needs to be spelt out in a formal constitution so that there are no misunderstandings about the sensitive area of the relation between plant and combine organizations.

Solidarity and plant autonomy
In order to build trust and solidarity across plants it is important that plant organizations do not feel dominated or manipulated by the wider combine. On the other hand in any campaign or struggle initiated or spread by the combine, the fight must come from the plants or else the combine is nothing.

Winning the argument: policies for social need
In a period of recession where according to management's arguments each plant is competing for resources, a combine committee will be very difficult to sustain unless it develops its own clear alternative policies for the industry. Policies which directly counter management's forecasts about falling markets by pointing to the social needs which remain unmet. Campaigns with a specific proposal based on social need help to puncture management's 'constraints' and develop the members' confidence that there *is* an

alternative worth fighting for. Such policies also help to win wider support to save jobs – from workers in other sectors and from the wider community.

Research and information resources

The ideas for such policies will come from within our own organizations. But to develop them and to be fully informed about management's strategies we need to work with researchers who have the time and resources to go into problems in more detail. In many areas local trade union research and resource centres have been created by researchers committed to the trade union movement, working closely with local shop-stewards' committees. These are a very important part of the growth of a more powerful shop-floor trade unionism. It is important that these research and resources centres are under the control of the local trade union movement; or where they are based in academic institutions that they are under joint academic/trade union control.

Co-ordination between combine committees

One feature of the increased power of top management is their greater co-ordination and mutual support. Trade unionists by contrast have not been organized in such a way as to give effective support to each other, across companies. Yet the problems we face in different companies are not only very similar, but are increasingly interconnected.

It is for these reasons that combine committees must not only extend and strengthen their support within plants but must build links between each other.

International contacts

The first practical objective of combine committees is to develop sufficient solidarity and understanding of top management's plans and manoeuvres, to be able to block off the range of options which give management its power. However effective our means of achieving this at home, most of our efforts can be undermined by the options available to management internationally; unless we build up an international network.

Such contacts and the information gathered through them, can help to overcome a feeling of helpnessness in the face of mysterious 'international economic forces'. Also when shop-stewards and members know something of the problems faced by workers in the company's plants abroad, when they can put faces and familiar problems to management's statistics, it is more difficult to play off the international plants against the domestic ones.

Trade unionism across frontiers

In this last section we look at the possibilities of 'internation-alizing' the work of trade union organization in general and combine committees in particular.

International monopolies

Below we reproduce extracts from three news stories which appeared in the press on one day in 1980. Imagine yourself a worker employed in one of the industries or companies referred to. How could you and your workmates react as an organization to the issues raised in these reports?

'In Detroit some 250,000 plus car workers are currently in the dole queues.'

'Allegheny Ludlum has won the support of the Wilkinson Match directors (a British-based company) in a deal valuing the group at £53.5 million. The American company has bumped up the offer price to 187p per share from the 168p suggested in early July. . . The WM employees have been reassured about jobs: no redundancies are foreseen as a consequence of the acquisition.'

'Atlantic Richfield, owners of the *Observer* newspaper, yesterday reported a 71 per cent increase in earnings for the first six months of the year. . . Dismissal notices were sent to more than 1000 *Observer* employees yesterday and the paper announced that its last edition would appear on 19 October. The NGA . . . are in dispute with the management over the payment of machine managers.'

All three reports illustrate how decisions affecting workers in Britain are not necessarily made in Britain. We referred to the growth and development of the big international conglomerates in Chapter two.

Giant multinational companies have become an increasingly characteristic form of business organization. Remember Maggie and Dennis? Dennis worked for Mono Pumps, an engineering firm, part of the Gallaher tobacco empire. According to the 1979 *Who Owns Whom?* Gallaher directly controlled seventy-five companies in the UK *and* owned subsidiaries in the Netherlands, Italy, Republic of Ireland, Federal Republic of Germany, South Africa, Australia, Canada and the USA. In turn Gallaher is controlled by the giant US corporation, American Brands Inc.

Gallaher, then, is a 'multinational company', an enterprise which makes direct investments in more than one country and which sees both its day-to-day management and its long-term strategy from an international point of view.

What are the issues for trade unionists? Multinationals pose the following problems for trade unionists

● Trade unions find it difficult to identify who makes decisions. Is it local management, or is it international head office? The local subsidiary management of multinational companies has been characterized as an essentially powerless puppet which dances to the tune of the international and non-national headquarters management.

● Trade unions fear multinational companies will import industrial relations practices which undermine existing trade union organization. When the American management closed down the Roberts-Arundel engineering works in Stockport in 1968 after a long and bitter dispute, they returned to the United States, in the words of one of their managers, to operate much more easily without having the unions on our backs.

● Trade unions fear the loss of job security. By 1980 at least 15 per cent of all jobs in Britain were with subsidiaries of multinational companies. The threat to transfer production elsewhere has become a potent form of blackmail as many workers know only too well. As the *Financial Times* reported some years ago: 'there is a developing trend for Western Europe to serve as a stop-over for American investment on the way to the developing world where production costs and social legislation do not bear comparison with those of European countries'. Figure 7 is only one example of the cheap labour cost advantage of investing in the developing world.

Matching the power of the multinationals International co-operation amongst trade unionists has increased as

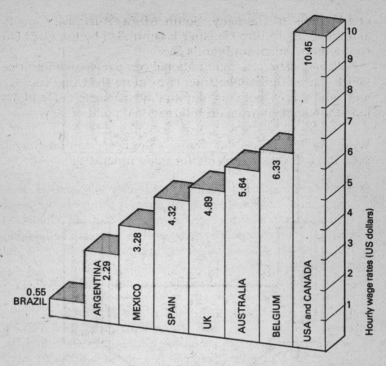

Figure 7 Wages of floor-sweepers employed by Ford around the world
Ford World Auto Council, 1980

workers have begun realizing that multinational companies can only be countered by trade union action which is itself multinational. Determining a strategy towards the multinationals is no easy task, for international trade union solidarity has to overcome all sorts of administrative, cultural and political difficulties. The political barriers to international action are coming down and, given time, other problems will be resolved.

One strategy which has attracted growing support has been put forward by Charles Levinson, General Secretary of the International Chemical, Energy and Allied Workers Federation (ICF) – one of a number of trade union 'internationals'

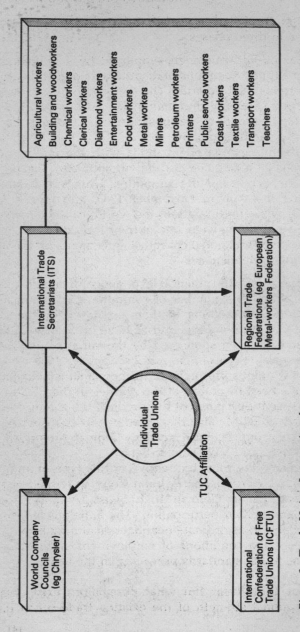

Figure 8 Trade Union Internationals

(see Figure 8). He has argued that the trade union response should be in three phases:

● All unions with members employed by a multinational giving support to unions in dispute with one of the company's foreign subsidiaries. The support to be extended to affect the company multinationally. Also support might be given by unions in the subsidiaries to a union in dispute with the parent company.

● Open simultaneous negotiations with the multinational company in a number of different countries. Establish a permanent co-ordinating committee. Thus Ford car unions meeting in Spain in November 1980, and representing 500,000 workers throughout the world, called for making a shorter working week one of their top priorities.

● Conclude international collective agreements on the basis of common demands.

As yet there is little practical experience of applying this strategy, although a number of committees and councils of trade unions representing workers employed by the same multinational in different countries have been formed. Most initiatives have been sponsored by the various trade union 'internationals'. For example, on 2 December 1980 clothing and textile unions throughout Europe held simultaneous one-hour actions in protest at the policies of the EEC in the face of the continuing loss of hundreds of thousands of jobs. The International Metalworkers' Federation sponsors World Automative Councils for Chrysler, General Motors, Ford, Toyota-Nissan and VW/Daimler-Benz.

But perhaps the most impressive of this type of initiative is the Michelin World Trade Union Council, formed in 1971 with French, Italian, German, Irish, Swiss, Canadian, Algerian and Argentinian participation. The aims of the Council in general are to co-ordinate negotiations and strike support and to raise the conditions of employment in all Michelin operations to the standards prevailing in the best.

Shop-floor initiatives But what possibilities exist outside the institutional strength of the existing trade union internationals? After all that kind of support has not, and will not, always be there. What are the possibilities for shop-stewards to develop international support?

The task of building international links outside the existing trade union internationals presents tremendous problems for shop-stewards. Initial contacts must be made, language and cultural differences must be broken down, and regular meetings have to be organized and financed – the latter mostly from the pockets of those taking part. But there have been some impressive examples of international co-operation at shop-floor level. Dockers and seamen on both sides of the Channel on the Newhaven-Dieppe ferries have co-operated closely for a number of years producing tangible and practical results. Vauxhall stewards at Ellesmere Port have sought co-operation from German and American trade unionists in opposing General Motors' redundancy proposals.

The Dunlop-Pirelli International Steering Committee has brought together workplace representatives from the company's plants in Italy, Britain and France since 1971. The famous 'Day of Struggle', 9 June 1972, saw co-ordinated strike action by 25,000 Italian and 14,000 British workers against the company's rationalization plans.

International solidarity in action: The Cimolai case It is difficult to imagine a more hostile environment to international trade union co-operation than United States Air Force bases in East Anglia. But during the summer of 1978 events unfurled which brought a remarkable victory for international trade union solidarity.

In the early months of 1978 the first phase of aircraft shelter construction at the Suffolk USAF bases of Lakenheath, Bentwaters, Woodbridge and Alconbury was nearing completion. The main contractor on the site was Costains. An important site sub-contractor to Costains was Cimolai, a steel fabricating firm from Pordenone in Northern Italy. Cimolai had experienced financial difficulties on phase one and announced that for phase two it intended to introduce Italian labour.

A second site sub-contractor, Carter Horseley, also claimed heavy financial losses on phase one and on 14 July 1978 announced that as from the following Monday, wages for piece-work and time-rated work would be drastically reduced. They announced that those workers willing to accept the wage cut would be re-employed on 17 July but for those unwilling to accept it was down the road. Altogether eighty-five steel erectors, welders and platers, members of the AUEW Construction Section, stood to lose their jobs through the actions of the sub-contractors.

The ultimatum was tantamount to a lock-out and a dispute which was to last fourteen weeks began. The strike committee immediately called on the UCATT and TGWU members on site to black any work with the steel erecting contract. Their request was met in full. The dispute dragged on for five weeks until at the end of August Carter Horseley and Cimolai began to ship in non-unionized Italian labour. Despite intensive picketing, the Italian strike-breakers gained access to the bases. The strike committee successfully appealed to the UCATT and TGWU members on site not to work alongside the Italians. It was also decided to stop all contractors from delivering to the sites and to appeal to haulage workers and dockers not to handle any goods destined for the bases. Complete support came from Felixstowe and Ipswich dockers and road haulage drivers. But still there was no end to the dispute in view. The strike committee began to realize that British trade union support alone would be insufficient to win. They decided therefore on a direct appeal to Italian trade unionists. A telephone call was made to the international office of the Italian Metalworkers Union in Rome requesting immediate intervention and support. On 4 September the Italian union sent a telegram to the General Secretary of the AUEW Construction Section pledging full support. Four days later the AUEW Construction Section executive declared the strike official, making it clear that they 'would shut down every construction site in Britain unless Italian scab labour was withdrawn'.

On the same day the strike committee printed leaflets and posters in English and Italian for distribution in Britain and Italy. The leaflets called on Italian workers:

'. . . to demonstrate international trade union solidarity and not to allow Italy to be used as a base for the assembly of mobile squads of strike-breakers within the EEC and to act in order to defeat the machinations of employers transcending national frontiers.'

On 11 September Italian trade union officials flew to Britain for consultation with the AUEW Construction Section and confrontation with the site contractors. While British and Italian union officials met Costains and Cimolai management, Cimolai workers in Italy staged a one-hour strike to show their solidarity with their British colleagues.

Costains were now faced with a possible shutdown of all their British construction sites; Cimolai were coming under increasing pressure in Italy and facing daily confrontation on the picket line in Britain. Together they took the decision to 'temporarily' withdraw the scabs 'to allow time for further negotiations'. Pressure on the contractors was intensified. Sympathy strikes were called at seventeen construction sites – from Tilbury to Humberside, from South Kirby to Ponders End.

The employers finally cracked. On 17 October negotiations took place and a settlement acceptable to the men was reached. Under the agreement:

- Each worker was to receive £1400 tax free, as compensation for the lock-out period.
- Each worker would be re-employed by a new site contractor, Robert Stevenson Ltd, on wages and conditions no worse than those prevailing prior to the start of the dispute.
- All the phase two work would be done by the existing work-force, which meant a guarantee of employment for fourteen months.

This dispute was remarkable for the resourcefulness of the workers involved. 'Official' trade union support had been sought and won; sympathetic action at local level by fellow site workers, dockers and lorry drivers, at national level by fellow construction workers, and at international level by Italian trade unionists had been achieved. As the strike committee commented a couple of months after the dispute:

The vital lesson for all trade unionists is the need to forge and strengthen links at rank and file level, locally, regionally, nationally and internationally.

Is trade union action enough?

Even if trade union organization was developed across frontiers in the way we have suggested would that in itself be enough to control the activities of multinational companies? In the same way that the trade union movement in Britain formed the Labour Party for the purpose of advancing the interests of working people on a political level (through Parliament), so trade unions see the necessity of control (through legislation) of the multinationals. The political attack has been developed along two lines, firstly, sponsoring national legislation aimed at restricting multinational power, and secondly, supporting international regulation through various international bodies.

National legislation

The big emphasis here has been on preventing the export of jobs. In Sweden, for example, the metalworkers' union (engineers) led a campaign in the early 1970s which forced the Swedish Department of Industry to assume the task of preventing investments abroad which would be against the interests of the economy. In addition the government has added a 'social code' to their investment guarantee programme which requires multinational companies to 'recognize trade unions . . . enter into collective bargaining according to the host country's rules . . . (and) . . . give the union notice of lay-offs and facilitate the adjustment of workers laid off'.

International regulation

The idea of some form of international code of conduct on the activities of multinational companies was first put forward by the international trade union movement in the late 1960s. Since then a number of possible approaches have been suggested. What they have in common is a central role for intergovernmental organizations like the United Nations, the International Labour Organization (ILO) and the EEC. The most widely accepted approach is the 'Charter on the Multinationals' adopted by the International Confederation of Free Trade Unions (ICFTU) in 1975. It calls on intergovernmental organizations to take necessary steps to have international agreements adopted in the following seven areas:

● dissemination of information;
● companies' social obligations;
● monitoring of international direct investment and changes taking place in company ownership;
● restrictive commercial practices such as price fixing;
● taxation of the multinationals;
● technology transfers;
● short-term movements of capital.

So far little progress has been made. The EEC for example has been unwilling to go further than recognize that measures should be adopted to 'protect the workers' interests' from the more pernicious activities of multinationals. As yet no intergovernmental body has in any meaningful way proceeded beyond the stage of pious declarations.

Further reading

Two other books in this series are essential complementary reading: Alan Campbell and John McIlroy, *Getting Organized*, (Pan Books, 1981). Chris Baker and Peter Caldwell, *Unions and Change Since 1945* (Pan Books, 1981).

The best recent general survey is Ken Coates and Tony Topham, *Trade Unions in Britain* (Spokesman).

Two other useful books are Daryll Hull, *Shop Stewards Guide to Work Organization* (Spokesman) and Tony Topham, *The Organized Worker* (Arrow).

On combine committees essential reading is *Trade Union Strategy in the Face of Corporate Power* (CAITS).

Chapter Six

Why it's still an
uphill struggle

We've suggested in Chapters four and five that certain courses of action are open to trade unionists which would allow them greater influence at work. In particular we've concentrated on extending collective bargaining objectives and strengthening trade union organization.

But are there limits to what trade union action alone can achieve? Are there external factors at play which restrain the ability of the trade union movement to go forward in extending workplace power? Are there issues outside the control of trade unionists which have a fundamental impact on our

147

working lives? This final chapter tries to provide some answers to these questions.

Haven't we got enough problems with unemployment?

Let's begin by looking at the issue which dominates so many radio and television news broadcasts and attracts banner headlines day after day in the national press – Britain's economic problems. In December 1980 the Organization for Economic Co-operation and Development (OECD) – a major forum for the big capitalist nations of the world – had this to say about the development of the British economy for the period to mid-1982:

● Unemployment at three million;
● Inflation at 9 per cent;
● An annual balance of payments deficit of $6,000 million;
● A fall in national output of 2 per cent;
● A fall in manufacturing investment of 13 per cent;
● A fall in industrial output to 1965 levels.

A gloomy prospect, yet one which does no more than reflect the fears of hundreds of thousands of men and women who at best face a real decline in their standards of living, and at worst the spectre of the dole queue.

The causes of the current recession are many. Some have a British dimension alone, such as the failure of industry and government to invest in and plan for the future of British industry. Others are of a world dimension, such as the collapse of the international monetary system, the escalating price of primary products, particularly oil, and the way multinational companies ride roughshod over the international economy. The consequences are clear – particularly for jobs.

The crude figures of unemployment are by themselves an indictment of economic mismanagement. Whereas they cannot disguise the human waste involved, they say little about the nature of the demoralization and misery caused. 'Suicide, stress, alcoholism, deteriorating sex-life, violence, murder and other crimes, mental illness and heart disease' constituted one report's short-list of the possible effects of losing your job. Another research project showed that a rise in unemployment of one million spread over five years would bring with it an increase of more than 50,000 in the expected number of deaths – with 700 of these being caused by extra suicides and 130 by extra murders. Over the same period, mental illness would increase by 63,900 cases, and prison sentences by 13,900.

The impact of new technology is one of the most alarming features of this present crisis. Again forecasts for the future are horrifying. ASTMS has estimated that by 1985 the number of information workers in the economy will have reached 50 per cent and will be of a similar proportion in 1991. On the assumption that the job displacement effects of new information technology on information workers is 20 per cent in 1985 and 30 per cent by 1991, and that the unemployment rate among non-information workers is 10 per cent in both 1985 and 1991, the union estimates there will be 3,831,000 unemployed by 1985, an unemployment rate of 15 per cent, and 5,235,000 unemployed by 1991, an unemployment rate of 20 per cent.

Reports of how this is working through in practice are now commonplace. In 1980, for example, the telecommunications side of the Plessey group shed 2500 workers – workers with skills in making pre-computer telephone equipment. Their jobs have now been automated. This has had nothing to do with the recession because business is booming in telecommunications. Indeed Plessey's telecommunications operation has increased its profits in two years by 73 per cent. Also its wage bill has risen because the company has taken on 1600 more highly paid staff, including computer programmers, electronic technicians, accountants and marketing specialists.

In general terms it has been suggested that the occupations most likely to be affected by the introduction of new technology would include:

● clerical;
● processing, making, repairing (metal and electronic);

- painting, repetitive assembly, product inspecting and packaging;
- making and repairing (excluding metal and electrical);
- management (excluding general management);
- professionals in science, engineering and technology;
- materials processing (excluding metals);
- selling.

In Chapter three we saw how new technology can mean increased managerial control and changes in workplace practices behind the screen of technological necessity. It is also clear how new technology poses a threat to jobs. In such circumstances, therefore, any trade union response must draw together the relationship between control at work and the following areas:

- economic investment;
- profits and the management function;
- new technology;
- unemployment.

How then should the trade union movement respond? Firstly, let's look at the possibilities which union collective bargaining aims offer.

As a first response trade unionists should resist the introduction of new technology until assurances have been won about jobs. At local level the TGWU, for example, has suggested that this must be translated into special agreements between unions and employers which specify a joint procedure covering the following points:

- New technology will only be introduced by mutual agreement, backed by a 'status quo' condition.
- All relevant information must be made available to trade union negotiators.
- No enforced redundancies as a result of introducing new technology.
- Changes in the deployment of workers or in shift working only to be made by mutual agreement.
- Any changes in skills or working practices to be reflected in improved wage levels.

- Full training and retraining of any workers affected by the introduction of new technology.
- Full trade union involvement on all aspects of health and safety procedures before any new technology is introduced.
- New technology must not be used to collect information on individual or collective work measurement.
- All the above questions must be subject to regular review to monitor the effects of new technology.

Secondly, the introduction of new technology and the fight for control gives trade unionists the opportunity to raise the issue of the quality of working life. Trade unionists should press for much greater flexibility into arrangements for going to work. Furthermore, the time each individual spends at work must be reduced. This could mean reduced overtime, a shorter working week, increased holiday entitlement, earlier retirement and work sharing. Workers' time which is 'released' like this could make a major contribution to wresting some control from management. What we are suggesting here is that time reclaimed from manager-controlled work could be used to monitor and plan trade union alternatives to management strategies. In practical terms it might mean a more widespread involvement and commitment to trade union meetings, conferences, courses and research activities.

Any large cuts in working time suggests that ultimately consideration must be given to the possibility of a minimum income level for everyone, which would not necessarily be derived exclusively from employment. This would have profound economic and social implications. As ASTMS has argued:

. . . this would mean changes in lifestyle and patterns of work. We should consider the availability of meaningful alternatives to paid work, opportunities to move in and out of formal employment arrangements in the course of a working life, different mixes of paid and unpaid work and leisure activity, much greater recourse to work-sharing and, within the household, a different allocation of work and family responsibilities. A suitable social objective would be to expand the range of combinations of employment income and

151

nonemployment activities from which the individual can choose in the course of a lifetime.

Aren't new national policies required?

But, you may ask, aren't these questions which have to be settled at the top? How can trade unionists at the workplace press for policies which suggest a total rethink of the way work is organized? Isn't this a role for the TUC, or for the Labour Party? And in any case aren't you raising *political* questions?

Indeed these are political questions and have been recognized as such by individual trade unions and the TUC. Because government decisions can affect the lives of workers it is to be expected that trade unions will attempt to influence the decisions governments make. Within the context of the current recession the TUC has vigorously campaigned for alternative economic policies to be pursued. In 1979, the year the present Conservative Government came into office, the TUC called for a positive economic strategy which would include:

● Measures to strengthen the economic base, including the strategic use of North Sea oil and gas revenue and effective policies against import penetration.
● Major advances in industrial democracy and a strengthening of the effectiveness of the industrial strategy.
● Taxation policies which promote the achievement of stable prices.
● Recognition of the indispensable part which pensions, child benefits and the education, health and other public services play in the social wage.
● Recognition of the increasingly vital role of public enterprise and public investment.

More recently the TUC, in its 1981 Economic Review, put forward a plan for national recovery. It argued that a massive investment programme was necessary to rebuild the economy. In particular it called for major public sector investment projects in transport and housing, in telecommunications and energy. It also identified the need for a properly co-ordinated national planning system, involving a revitalized National Enterprise Board and the establishment of a National Investment Bank. The costs of such a plan could be met by the more effective use of North Sea oil revenues and reducing the appalling cost of unemployment. In the immediate term the TUC called for a £6 billion programme of investment to get the economy moving forward again. Predictably the Conservative Government turned down the advice. The cost of not adopting these measures, according to the TUC's calculations, is a million more on the dole queue.

But the members aren't interested

We expect that many of you will agree with the arguments presented here, but you know from your own experience how difficult it can be to convince others. The only way forward is to continue to argue for the right kind of policies. But if these are to have any chance of being implemented, discussion and debate must not remain confined to national forums. In clubs, pubs and especially workplaces, the debate has to go on so that workers can be fully mobilized behind a programme which reflects their workplace needs and their broader interests as members of the trade union movement.

It's not going to be easy. There are powerful vested interests standing in the way. Government and employers will be quick to resist any attempts to place the interests of workers and their families above their own. Press, radio and television have rarely shown sympathy or understanding for issues pursued by workers and their unions. And it would be foolish in the extreme to underestimate how demoralized many sections of workers are as a result of the worst recession experienced in Britain since the 1930s.

Don't be surprised then if your first attempts to get some discussion going are met by apathy, disinterest or downright hostility. You're up against powerful opposition and progress will be tough.

But there is a way forward and it lies in bravely confronting the issues which affect you and your workmates in factory, office or hospital within the context of the broad themes we've discussed in this book – the 'who', 'why' and 'how' of control at work. Let's take a practical example of how one group of workers addressed themselves to these questions.

In 1976 Lucas Aerospace shop-stewards unveiled their Corporate Plan for the company in which they proposed an alternative and more socially desirable product range designed to combat the threat of redundancies. The plan called for the introduction of new products in a phased manner so that the tendency for the industry to contract would first be halted and then gradually reversed as Lucas Aerospace diversified into new fields of production.

Lucas Aerospace Ltd is a wholly owned subsidiary of the British-based multinational, Lucas Industries Ltd. It is Europe's largest designer and manufacturer of aircraft systems and equipment and when the plan was presented employed some 13,000 workers at seventeen plants in the UK.

The drawing up of the Corporate Plan was the direct result of the continuous threat to jobs. Fear of rationalization within the company, accompanied by substantial redundancies, had led in 1969 to the formation of the Lucas Aerospace and Defence Systems shop-stewards combine committee. In the early '70s the combine established various advisory services for the membership including a Pensions Advisory Service and a Science and Technology Advisory Service. The Corporate Plan was prepared as part of the combine's long-term strategy of resistance to redundancies.

In broad terms there were two objectives to the Plan:

● To protect the right to work by proposing a range of alternative products on which workers could become engaged in the event of cutbacks in the industry.
● To ensure that among the alternative products proposed were a number which would be socially useful to the community at large.

All told some 150 alternative products were proposed of which twelve were selected to form the first package for 'presentation' to management. These twelve products were suitable for use in the following major areas of technology:

154

- Oceanics
- Telechiric (remote control) machines
- Transport systems
- Braking systems
- Alternative energy sources
- Medical equipment

There is a gap between what technology *can* provide and what it actually *does* provide in meeting human problems and needs and the Lucas stewards exposed this by concentrating on socially useful products.

They argued that 'scientists, engineers and the workers in these industries have a profound responsibility to challenge the underlying assumptions of large scale industry; seek to assert their right to use their skill and ability in the interest of the community at large'.

The combine's emphasis on production for social need before profit represented a challenge to the way business normally operates. Business is at the heart of the political system and certainly the Lucas stewards recognized that they were making a political challenge. This is how they saw it:

Perhaps the most significant feature of the Corporate Plan is that trade unionists are attempting to transcend the narrow economism which has characterized trade union activity in the past and extend our demands to the extent of questioning the products on which we work and the way in which we work upon them.

As an essential complement to arguing for socially useful products the combine demanded the rehumanizing of jobs. It noted that this century has seen systematic efforts to de-skill jobs, to fragment them into narrow functions and to have them carried out at increased speed. At Lucas 'attempts to replace human intelligence by machine intelligence . . . have had quite disastrous results. It is intended to campaign for quite radical job redesign which will protect our members from this.' That campaign would involve the introduction of an employee development programme which would particularly focus on four areas of special concern:

- The company had failed to extend or develop the skills and ability of the work-force.

155

- The age group in some of the plants was very high, typically around forty-six to fifty years average.
- There was little indication that the company was developing any real programme of apprenticeships.
- There was little evidence that the company was attempting to employ women in technical jobs.

Although since 1976 the company has displayed a marked lack of enthusiasm for the combine's proposals, they still remain on the combine's agenda. The combine has continued to press for socially useful work to be carried out within companies as a result of negotiation. It's backed up its arguments more recently by analysing the uses and misuses of public money pumped into Lucas and other companies, suggesting that if companies were made accountable for every penny of public money they received then socially useful product proposals would not only meet social needs but create more jobs.

It is clear that the Lucas combine's proposals challenge the very basis of modern industrial organization. In these proposals the profit motive is no longer the absolute god. The interests of workers and the needs of society as a whole come first. It is above all an argument for the more democratic control of industry.

Don't the unions disagree over industrial democracy?

We referred earlier in this chapter to the TUC's plan for national recovery. At the heart of the TUC's concept of effective planning lies the need to link planning of the economy as a whole with rapid advances in industrial democracy. More democratic control over what happens in the economy and in individual enterprises are therefore tightly linked demands.

By industrial democracy we mean extending the influence and activities of workplace trade union organization, and there can be no doubt that this can be achieved by a number of routes, such as extending collective bargaining. It is precisely because there are a number of ways forward that the subject has attracted considerable argument within the trade union movement.

For a period in the mid-1970s discussion turned on whether or not worker directors were an appropriate way forward. It was no accident that the debate was raised at this time. From the Upper Clyde Shipbuilders work-in of 1971, through so many factory occupations, to the formation of the workers' co-operatives at Meriden, Kirkby and the *Scottish Daily News* and the bringing down of the Heath Government in 1974, workers were questioning the way industry was run. It was said at the time that this was more than a challenge to 'management's right to manage', it was a challenge to 'capitalism's right to control'.

In this climate, employers were concerned to thwart any claims for democratic control and in many cases responded by offering the *appearance* of power-sharing through consultation and participation schemes. There was also another reason why employers began to show enthusiasm for greater participation. The early '70s saw the growth of short-time working and large-scale redundancies. Throughout whole sectors of the economy emphasis had been on rationalization, on increasing productivity and on reducing manning levels. Quite rightly employers expected the unions to resist the loss of jobs. But if in some way the unions could be identified with policy-making, then it would prove very difficult for them to oppose lay-offs if they had participated in the very process which had brought such a situation about.

The Labour Government, which came into office in 1974, was elected on a manifesto which included a commitment to legislate on industrial democracy as part of its broad industrial strategy for the 'regeneration of British industry'. Labour's Industry Act, and its shipbuilding and aircraft nationalization proposals gave trade unions important rights to disclosure of information. Also the concept of Planning Agreements and the setting up of the National Enterprise Board (NEB) suggested a much wider role for trade unions in economic decision-making. Later, a government White Paper, following the publication of the Bullock Report, promised to legislate for the introduction of worker directors.

The TUC's position on industrial democracy was outlined in the General Council's report to the 1974 Congress. It called for the trade union movement to work towards greater industrial democracy on the basis of the following general strategy:

- Trade union organization should be strengthened.
- Matters previously outside of collective agreements should become subject to negotiation.
- Information on the operations of the enterprise should be made available to workers and their representatives.
- Trade union parity representation on top boards of enterprises.

These recommendations were to signpost the main way forward for extending collective control at local level. But, in the TUC's view, this would leave a wide range of managerial decisions still beyond the control of workers. Therefore, the report argued, new forms of control, through representation at the point where decisions affecting workers were made, would be necessary. In line with this, proposals were put forward for union representation on company boards.

Could a similar approach be followed in the public sector? The report made it clear that if the proposals for worker representation in private industry were adopted, then similar forms of representation should be established within the nationalized industries and the public services. In relation to local government for example, NUPE was later to argue that 50 per cent of local councils should be elected by the voters and 50 per cent by the employees of the council. NALGO suggested that a workers' council should be elected from employees which would choose representatives to take up a minimum of four seats on every council and a maximum of 20 per cent on each council committee. NALGO again, perhaps with the BSC and Post Office worker director experiments very much in mind (see page 83), pressed for 50 per cent trade union representation on the gas industry board.

At the 1974 TUC Congress, debate focused on the worker director issue. It was clear that the General Council's support for workers on the board was unacceptable to large sections of the trade union movement. Eddie Marsden, from the AUEW Construction Section, represented the views of many delegates when he said:

It is precisely the growth and strength of the shop-stewards' movement that frightens big business . . . this may be one of the reasons why some sections (of big business) supported the worker director idea because of the obvious provision for conflict and frustration for our shop-stewards on the one hand, and to turn them into defenders of the system on the other.

The worker director debate was replayed at the 1975 and 1976 Congresses. But within the trade union movement attitudes were hardening against worker director proposals which were not complemented by a thorough reform of traditional company structures. When the Bullock Committee of Inquiry reported in 1977, proposing only minority representation for worker directors, many trade unionists felt the same way as the delegate from the Society of Post Office Executives who, at the 1975 TUC, had predicted that:

We shall be used by the management as a Trojan horse to get our members to accept the sort of policies that the management knows it would not have a cat in hell's chance of getting through if it came to us during the normal course of collective bargaining.

Lukewarm support from the trade union movement for worker directors should not be interpreted as thumbs down to industrial democracy. The two issues are separate. The commitment to industrial democracy remains as strong as ever, particularly in the role collective bargaining can play in extending workers' control over their work.

If we see industrial democracy as a sharing of power by workers in decisions which were previously the responsibility of management alone, then the whole history of the trade union movement has been the history of extending industrial democracy. In this sense, extending collective bargaining is the key element in industrial democracy and is recognized as such by the trade union movement. It is in this sense as well that extending collective bargaining can play a central role in national economic planning. This is how the TUC's 1981 Economic Review drew these two questions together:

There is a wider, more constructive role for collective bargaining in the TUC's plan for recovery. Trade union objectives – including greater job security, the elimination of low pay and shorter working time – need to be pursued at many levels. It is essential, however, that trade unionists continue, through collective bargaining and its further development, to pursue such objectives directly. The TUC's campaign for reduced working time, for example, has been highly successful in achieving shorter working time across the economy. This is a major and distinctive trade union contribution to the balance of economic development since it lays a basis for ensuring that future productivity growth will be channelled into increased employment rather than unequally distributed benefits. This is a clear example of the scope for direct trade union inputs to a process of planned economic recovery.

So where do we go from here?

The ways in which workers press for greater democracy at work have always been determined by the circumstances of their time. In the formative years of the trade union movement the priority was survival against the opposition of employers and state alike. But because of the courage and solidarity shown by workers, trade unionism survived and built up its strength throughout the nineteenth century. The twentieth century has witnessed a formidable growth in support for trade unionism, but again it has not been achieved without considerable sacrifice or periods of reverse and defeat. What remains constant, irrespective of time or circumstances, is the basic objective of trade unionism – to achieve for working people and their families a greater say in those matters which directly affect them.

Seventy years ago one group of workers saw the issues like this:

So long as the system of working for wages endures, collective bargaining remains essential . . . (the men realize) that collective bargaining can be made so wide-reaching and all embracing, that it includes the whole of the working class. In this form the employers . . . have no love for it . . . because they realize its dangers to their profits.

Today, as this book has shown, the same fundamental ques-

The Miners' Next Step, South Wales Miners' Reform Committee, 1912

tions confront the trade union movement. Industry is owned and controlled not by you, but by your employer; it is run not by you, but by management in the interests of the employer. We have suggested a number of ways in which trade unionists can begin to challenge this system of control; by seeking to bargain over issues which have been traditionally management's exclusive preserve and by ensuring that at the workplace trade unionism is organizationally strong enough to defend and advance workers' interests.

More than at any time since the war the economic climate is hostile to real progress. But however difficult the circumstances, the possibility remains for carrying forward the fight for industrial democracy. Jobs will remain the key issue for trade unionists for some time to come, so wherever trade unionists campaign over jobs the connection must be drawn between this issue and the issue of control at work. This can be done by pursuing practical policies which not only save and create jobs but which give workers a greater say in the decisions which previously have been management's alone.

In campaigning to cut working hours, to protect workers against abuses of technological change, and in pressing for alternatives to redundancy, the possibility exists for trade unionists to rebuild their confidence and press on for greater democracy at work.

Further reading

A valuable starting point for considering the issues raised in this chapter within their economic and political context is the *1981 TUC Economic Review*. As part of its Campaign for Economic and Social Advance the TUC has published a number of useful booklets. For a full list write to the Publications Department, TUC, Congress House, Great Russell Street, London WC1.

The Institute for Workers Control (IWC) also publishes many useful pamphlets. For a list write to IWC, Bertrand Russell House, Gamble Street, Nottingham.

Two other books in this series are again useful complementary reading: Alan Campbell and John McIlroy, *Getting Organized* (Pan Books 1981). Chris Baker and Peter Caldwell, *Unions and Change Since 1945* (Pan Books, 1981).

CAITS (Centre for Alternative Industrial and Technological Systems) provides much support material for developing trade union responses to unemployment. For a full list of their publications write to CAITS, North East London Polytechnic, Longbridge Road, Dagenham, Essex, RM8 2AS.

Index